First published in 2017 by Lund Humphries
in association with the Iris and B. Gerald Cantor
Center for Visual Arts, Stanford University

Lund Humphries
Office 3, Book House
261a City Road
London
EC1V 1JX

www.lundhumphries.com

Design for the Corporate World: 1950–1975
© Iris and B. Gerald Cantor Center for Visual
Arts, Stanford University, 2017
Essays © individual contributors, 2017

ISBN: 978-1-84822-194-9

A Cataloguing-in-Publication record for this book
is available from the British Library

Edited by Eleanor Rees
Designed by Zoë Bather
Set in Benton Gothic, Rockwell, Franklin Gothic
Printed in China

DESIGN FOR THE CORPORATE WORLD 1950–1975

EDITED BY WIM DE WIT

LUND HUMPHRIES
IN ASSOCIATION WITH
THE IRIS AND B. GERALD CANTOR CENTER FOR VISUAL ARTS, STANFORD UNIVERSITY

007   FOREWORD

008   ACKNOWLEDGMENTS

011   INTRODUCTION

139   BIOGRAPHIES OF MAJOR
         DESIGNERS REPRESENTED
         IN THE EXHIBITION
         CREATIVITY ON THE LINE

147   MAJOR CORPORATIONS
         INCLUDED IN THE EXHIBITION
         CREATIVITY ON THE LINE

154   NOTES

157   PHOTO CREDITS

158   INDEX

014
CLAIMING ROOM FOR CREATIVITY

THE CORPORATE DESIGNER & IDCA
WIM DE WIT

040
ESTABLISHMENT MODERNISM & ITS DISCONTENTS

IDCA IN THE 'LONG SIXTIES'
GREG CASTILLO

060
BUILDING MODERNIST BUT NOT QUITE

CORPORATE DESIGN IN THE POSTWAR SUBURB
LOUISE A. MOZINGO

084
DESIGN EDUCATION AT STANFORD

THE FORMATIVE YEARS
STEVEN McCARTHY

094
MAJOR OBJECTS IN THE EXHIBITION *CREATIVITY ON THE LINE*

round cotrese   9/20

7/31

maybe be out here

FOREWORD

The Cantor Arts Center at Stanford University is thrilled to present *Design for the Corporate World, 1950–1975*. Edited by Wim de Wit, The Cantor Arts Center's adjunct curator of Architecture and Design, this book and the exhibition (*Creativity on the Line: Design for the Corporate World 1950–1975*) it accompanies, are fitting for Stanford, where design has long played an important role, both in the physical appearance of the campus and in the courses taught throughout the university. While design education, by nature, is looking ahead toward the creation of new products, an examination of the past is also necessary in order to appreciate how the previous conditions that once governed design conception and execution are still imbedded in the professional work environment that exists today.

Presenting objects commonly identified with mid-century modernism in graphic, industrial, and architectural design, the book and exhibition seek to do more than highlight a stylistically unified group of objects. *Creativity on the Line* also, and perhaps more importantly, invites the viewer to consider the circumstances that made it possible for design to flourish during the 1950s and 60s, a period when a whole range of products that had been unavailable during the war years were brought back to the market, and when national and international corporations felt compelled to create unique identities so that they could promote those products in the booming economy. The authors of this edited volume look at these circumstances, examining both the opportunities and the drawbacks they presented to designers of corporate logos, advertisements, and mass-produced objects. We are pleased that the book also contains a chapter about the early history of Stanford's design program, which became the foundation for this university's renowned Hasso Plattner Institute of Design (better known as the d.school).

Creativity on the Line represents a new initiative for the Cantor Arts Center. It is our hope that this book and exhibition will generate lively discussion about the status of the designer and about design education in the United States both in the recent past and today, when the corporation is no longer considered to be the controlling institution designers once imagined it to be, and the fear of compromising one's creativity by working for industry has all but disappeared. Today's discussions about the design profession will, therefore, be very different from those considered in this book. They will, however, undoubtedly be just as revealing.

Matthew Tiews
Associate Dean for the Advancement of the Arts
Stanford University

Alison Gass
Chief Curator and Associate Director for Curatorial Affairs
Cantor Arts Center
Stanford University

ACKNOWLEDGMENTS

Museum exhibitions come about in many different ways. Very often, the project begins with an idea that a curator develops while researching a particular collection. Alternatively, the theme of an exhibition can be proposed by an outside scholar or expert who is then hired as a guest curator and, together with in-house staff, might bring the plan to fruition. The origin of *Creativity on the Line: Design for the Corporate World, 1950–1975* lies somewhere in between these two paradigms. During a meeting in early 2013 with Richard Saller, Stanford's Dean of the School of Humanities and Sciences, and Connie Wolf, former director of Stanford's Cantor Arts Center, I proposed to organize an exhibition based on research I had been doing in the archives of the International Design Conference in Aspen (IDCA), held at the Getty Research Institute in Los Angeles. Saller and Wolf both responded enthusiastically and, because the Cantor does not have an in-house design curator, offered me the temporary position of Adjunct Curator of Architecture and Design, which I eagerly accepted. I am grateful to Dean Saller for his support of my proposal, making it possible for me to conduct further research on the topic and shape the exhibition concept as a member of the Stanford community.

I also want to thank Connie Wolf for agreeing to present the exhibition at the Cantor and for accepting me as a staff member at her museum. Alison Gass, Chief Curator and Associate Director for Curatorial Affairs, and all other staff members have been most welcoming to me from the moment I arrived at the Cantor in September 2013. I want to express my thanks to all of them, not only for accepting me as a colleague, but especially for the assistance they have given to me and for making the work on the exhibition such a pleasant task. I especially appreciate the work of Katie Clifford, Andrea Mode, and the preparators who made sure that the organization of the exhibition stayed on track and that its installation proceeded without a glitch.

The faculty of Stanford's Department of Art and Art History has been very supportive to me by commenting on my research and giving advice. I am thankful to Professors Fabio Barry, Mark Braude, Richard Meyer, and Camille Utterback, who attended a roundtable discussion in the spring of 2016, and who not only helped me to further shape the concept of the exhibition, but also graciously provided us with ideas for public programs and offered to incorporate the exhibition into some of the classes offered during the spring of 2017. On separate occasions, Professor Barry Katz of Stanford's d.school and Professor Fred Turner of the School of Communication also commented on the concept of the exhibition and offered useful guidance. Robert H. McKim, David Kelley, and Bernard Roth met with me for several hours to discuss the early history of Stanford's design program. I want to express my thanks to all of them for the time they spent in support of my project.

The faculty of the d.school allowed us to offer a pop-up class to Stanford's students. In November 2016, students and faculty discussed issues surrounding exhibition design and developed a schematic plan for the installation of the *Creativity on the Line* exhibition. I very much appreciate the support we received from Professor David Kelley, Charlotte Burgess Auburn, Tania Anaissie, Carissa Carter, and Mark Grundberg, and want to thank the students for their enthusiasm and dedication.

While researching the exhibition, I met John Blakinger and Sydney Simon, PhD students in Stanford's Department of Art and Art History, who kindly shared their own research with me and drew my attention to archival collections of which, in some cases, I was not previously aware. I am grateful to both of them for their intellectual generosity.

The debates held as part of the annual meetings of the International Design Conference in Aspen were an extremely important resource for the development of my exhibition concept. I want to express my gratitude not only to the director and staff of the Getty Research Institute for allowing me to continue my research in those papers after I left the Institute as an employee, but also to the IDCA board members and conference participants, who were willing to meet with me and discuss my exhibition concept. I especially want to thank Julian Beinart, Ralph Caplan, Dorothy Globus, the late Jane Thompson, Eli Noyes, Thane Roberts, Sylvia Lavin and Greg Lynn for their time and advice.

I also want to recognize the catalog authors, Greg Castillo, Louise Mozingo and Steven McCarthy, for their insightful contributions to this book and for making the time available to write their essays in spite of busy teaching schedules at their own institutions. My heartfelt thanks also go to Selina Her and Rose Lachman for the research and writing of the designer biographies and entries on the corporations represented in the exhibition and this book, as well as to Sam Klotz, who was a great research assistant, and Veronica Oliva for her work as the permissions editor.

Creativity on the Line consists entirely of loan objects. I am extremely grateful to all the lenders, who not only were willing to meet with me when I was in the research phase of the exhibition, but who also spent many hours on approving and preparing the loans for the exhibition. I want to thank the directors, curators, and registrars of: The Art Institute of Chicago, Chicago, IL; Busch-Reisinger Museum at the Harvard Art Museums in Cambridge, MA; Computer History Museum, Mountain View, CA; Cooper Hewitt Smithsonian Design Museum, New York, NY; Getty Research Institute, Los Angeles, CA; Hagley Museum and Library, Wilmington, DE; Los Angeles County Museum of Art, Los Angeles, CA; Minneapolis Institute of Art in Minneapolis, MN; Museum of Modern Art, New York, NY; Piraneseum, Lafayette, CA; RIT Libraries, Graphic Design Archive, Rochester Institute of Technology, Rochester, NY; San Francisco Museum of Modern Art, San Francisco, CA; J. Paul Leonard Library, Archives and Special Collections, San Francisco State University, San Francisco, CA; the Sara Little Turnbull Archive, Seattle, WA; Smithsonian American Art Museum in Washington, DC; Green Library, Stanford University, Stanford, CA; Phoebe A. Hearst Museum of Anthropology, University of California, Berkeley; and Library Special Collections, Young Research Library, University of California, Los Angeles.

I am extremely appreciative for the assistance and advice I received from Dorothy Dunn, Waverly Lowell, Jonathan Massey, Johnny Tran, and Claudia Weill.

Val Rose, Lucie Ewin, and Eleanor Rees at Lund Humphries accepted this book for publication and shepherded it through the process of editing, design, and printing. I want to express my gratitude to them for their confidence in and dedication to the project.

Finally, I would like to thank my wife, Nancy J. Troy, without whom I would not have ventured to the United States some 35 years ago, and certainly not to Stanford. I can't thank her enough for her love, support and encouragement throughout those years.

Wim de Wit, November 2016

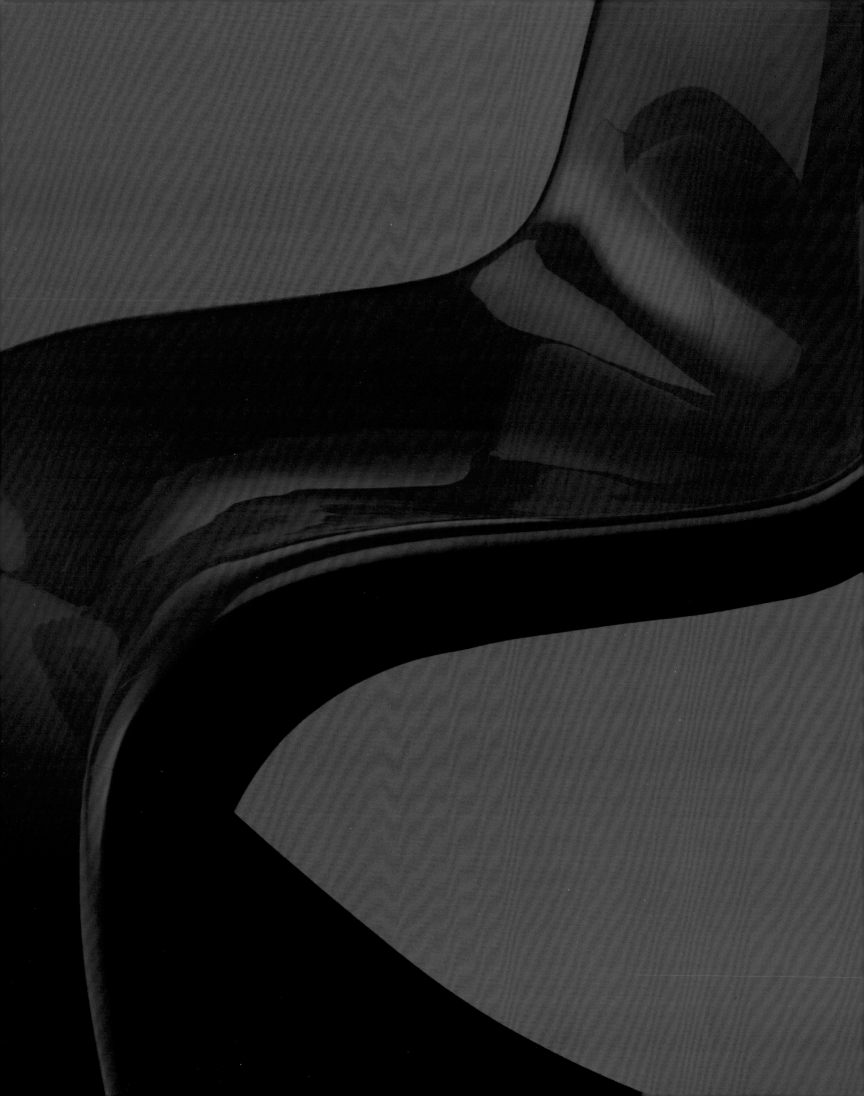

INTRODUCTION

Design for the Corporate World, 1950–1975 is a book about mid-century modern design. It presents the work of such famous artists as Saul Bass (see pl.10), Ivan Chermayeff (pl. 25 and 26), Charles and Ray Eames (pl.39), Eliot Noyes (ill.1.6 and pl.27), and Verner Panton (pl.40) whose creations are now included in most major collections of twentieth-century design. This book, however, is intended to be more than a monographic study devoted to the topic of design. Rather than highlighting individual careers or particular innovative products, this book looks specifically at the design profession in the third quarter of the twentieth century. It investigates the tensions that threatened to undermine the collaboration between corporate representatives on the one hand and, on the other hand, the designers whom they charged with creating compelling brands and products for mass consumption.

To a certain extent, this book is also an organizational history. A large part of the research for the book, and for the exhibition with which it is associated, was undertaken in the archives of the International Design Conference in Aspen (IDCA), which are housed at the Getty Research Institute in Los Angeles. IDCA, founded in 1951 by the Chicago industrialist Walter Paepcke, was a means to convince his fellow entrepreneurs that working with modern designers would be good for their businesses. The organization quickly became a meeting ground not so much for corporate managers but especially for designers who, while enjoying each other's company in a bucolic mountain setting where they discussed a wealth of different topics, could also share the concerns they felt about their relationship to the corporate world. The records of proceedings at the Aspen conferences are an excellent resource for learning about the nature of the design profession in the postwar period. They reveal a rich,

multidimensional spectrum of viewpoints that would be hard to come by if one were limited to examining the papers of individual designers, even ones who occasionally might have corresponded with one another.

Being a designer for the corporate world was not always a happy situation. The recurring question designers asked themselves was whether they should take on well-paying jobs in corporations led by managers who would not necessarily understand or appreciate design philosophies and therefore might force them to "water down" their creations; or whether they should maintain their status as independent artists and consequently forgo such lucrative jobs. No clear answers emerged from the discussions, but the IDCA archives time and again reveal designers' suspicions – not always expressed very clearly – that working for big business might jeopardize their creativity. Product designer Gordon Lippincott gave expression to the opinion of many of his colleagues when at the 1956 conference he exclaimed, "Management has, broadly speaking, not yet learned how to manage creative people in design." And as the drawings and objects illustrated in this book show (see, for example, Barnes and Reinecke's design for a juicer of c.1954, pl.48, and Garth Huxtable's design for a Millers Falls drill, n.d., pl.50), these designers were artists of excellence who valued the quality of a drawing and devoted a great deal of attention to thinking through both the functionality and the aesthetics of each detail of a product.

This book builds on such critically important studies as Reyner Banham's *The Aspen Papers: Twenty Years of Design Theory from the International Design Conference in Aspen* (New York and Washington, Praeger Publishers, 1974) and James Sloan Allen's *The Romance of Commerce and Culture: Capitalism, Modernism, and the Chicago-Aspen Crusade for Cultural Reform* (Chicago and London, The University of

"Design in an industrial organization is not a question of one brilliant idea, or even a series of creative bombshells. It is the slow permeation of a visual sensitivity through every aspect of the firm's work."

Mischa Black

Chicago Press, 1983). *The Aspen Complex* by Martin Beck, ed. (Berlin, The Sternberg Press, 2012), especially the chapter by Alice Twemlow, "'A Guaranteed Communications Failure:' Consensus meets Conflict at the International Design Conference in Aspen, 1970," which is an abbreviated version of a chapter in her dissertation "Purposes, Poetics, and Publics: The Shifting Dynamics of Design Criticism in the US and UK, 1955–2007" (London, Royal College of Art, 2013), has been of fundamental value as well. While these studies have proved to be indispensible resources, the book is not a history of IDCA. Instead, it mines the debates within that organization to build a foundation for a better understanding of the predicament in which the design profession found itself in the postwar period.

The first chapter of the present volume examines the ambivalence of designers about working for the corporate world through the lens of selected presentations at the Aspen design conferences. It also looks at certain political, economic, and cultural circumstances of the postwar period that encouraged corporations to become global entities in need of designers capable of making them stand out amongst their competitors. As the IDCA presentations of the 1950s, 60s and early 70s show, the opportunities created by these developments were received as mixed blessings by the designers who, in spite of the continuous flow of jobs coming from the corporate well, expressed doubts about the wisdom of taking them on. A position like that of Eliot Noyes at

IBM, where he was director of design and had the ear of CEO Thomas Watson, Jr., seems to have been an ideal solution, but nothing quite like it was available to most other designers.

Considering themselves to be artists, designers also thought of themselves as business people who were very much aware of what was going on in the "real" world. Still there were moments when that world presented itself abruptly, forcing them to think more carefully about their status in the corporate sphere, which was, of course, far from free of political and cultural influences. In Chapter Two, entitled "Establishment Modernism and Its Discontents: IDCA in the 'Long Sixties,'" Greg Castillo looks carefully at two IDCA conferences, the first of which took place in 1963 and the second in 1970. Taking as their themes "Design and the American Image Abroad" and "Environment by Design," respectively, these conferences became occasions for the Cold War and Northern California counterculture to interfere with the designers' image of themselves as modern and progressive intellectuals. The impact, especially of the 1970 conference, was huge. Liberal-minded, progressive design professionals suddenly saw themselves being aligned with the establishment. They did not know how to defend themselves against what they regarded as an underhanded attack. The tensions on display at this conference proved to be almost fatal to IDCA.

Louise Mozingo's chapter, "Building Modernist But Not Quite: Corporate Design in the Postwar Suburb," views the relationship between corporations and design from yet a different angle. While the book's first two essays examine the ambivalence felt by designers with respect to their place in the world, Mozingo's essay draws attention to the contradictions in the approach of the corporate directors, who on the one hand wanted their office buildings, and thus their companies, to look innovative and efficient as a result of designs commissioned from such high-modernist firms as Skidmore, Owings & Merrill (pl.29) or the office of Eero Saarinen, but who on the other hand did not necessarily embrace the relative starkness of modern architectural styles and therefore hired prominent landscape designers to soften the overall modernist effect. While this approach could have led to a schizophrenic result, in actuality it produced a number of stunning office complexes, especially on the east coast of the United States, that occupy large park-like settings and are well adapted to their suburban environment. The buildings and their surrounds became alternative icons to the downtown skyscraper and were able to maintain that position until very recently, when companies began moving back to the cities so many had left during the years following the war.

In the final chapter of the book, Steven McCarthy provides a brief history of design education at Stanford. It was at this university that in the late 1950s and early 1960s, key faculty from the Department of Mechanical Engineering and Department of Art and Architecture – notably John Arnold, Robert McKim and Matt Kahn – converged their interests in creativity, innovation, visual thinking, studio production and human-centeredness to build a joint graduate program in design. Emphasizing synthesis over analysis, problem-solving over style, and turning functional design projects into entrepreneurial ventures, Stanford's program evolved into an internationally respected enterprise. The legacy persists today with the extremely successful Hasso Plattner Institute of Design, better known as the d.school.

Misha Black, a well-known British designer, stated during the course of the 1956 IDCA conference:

> Design in an industrial organization is not a question of one brilliant idea, or even a series of creative bombshells. It is the slow permeation of a visual sensitivity through every aspect of the firm's work, from the product itself to the point of sales dispenser, from the architecture of the factory to the uniform of the truck driver, from the furnishing of the chairman's office to the fittings in the operatives' wash room.[1]

Black may have been thinking of Olivetti in Italy, or perhaps even Hille in his own country; both were companies that appreciated the work of designers and gave them more or less free rein. But in most other companies, however, their colleagues were not so fortunate. For them corporate work was a constant struggle, a struggle worth undertaking, but one that was frustrating nonetheless.

CLAIMING ROOM FOR CREATIVITY THE CORPORATE DESIGNER & IDCA

WIM DE WIT

The eleventh annual gathering of the International Design Conference in Aspen (IDCA) in summer 1961 was much less upbeat in tone than the preceding ten meetings had been.[1] Taken as a whole, the message conveyed by most of the speeches was quite dark, not so much about the current state of design, but about the dangerous world in which people felt they were living at the time. It is as if they were not particularly interested in talking about design. Conferees had to wait until the last day to hear even a single speaker make a significant point about the designer's role in the post-World War II economy and in particular about the pervasive fear of selling out to commerce. As we will see, world politics and questions of professional ethics were always on the designers' minds in the post-World War II era.

IDCA's "Man/Problem Solver" conference opened on Sunday, June 18, 1961, with a keynote address by Dr. Harold A. Taylor, a prolific writer on education and former president of Sarah Lawrence College (1945–59) who, during the McCarthy era, had distinguished himself through his support for members of the college's faculty accused of anti-American activities. In his 1961 Aspen lecture, Taylor told his audience, "The problem at the center of all other problems is war and peace," and he proceeded to speak out against the danger of nuclear war and mass destruction. He added: "The world's problem is now ours, and unless we take the lead in solving it creatively, there will be no more problems to solve." Taylor was not the only one to express such concerns. Anatol Rapoport, a Russian-American professor of Mathematical Biology at the University of Michigan in Ann Arbor, declared that the governments of the United States and the Soviet Union were apparently unable to solve urgent, large-scale problems in the world – the problem of hunger, for example – because government functionaries were trained only in strategic thinking and therefore unprepared to tackle the complex issues that demanded engagement at the higher, more demanding level of creative thinking. On a related note, the architect and social critic Bernard Rudofsky provoked his audience in characteristic fashion by asking if most humans would actually be able to recognize a problem if they saw one, and by making such outrageous statements as "any country without eroded soil and steaming dumps, without polluted rivers and polluted air we refer to, pityingly, as an underdeveloped country." Finally, on the last day of the conference, during the closing discussion, it was Bernard S. Benson, a British-American inventor and engineer working in the aviation industry, who refocused the debate on what was undoubtedly a core issue for the conferees when he observed, "The dilemma of the designer these days is 'How can I have my cake and eat it?' Though he may not want to admit it, he is really saying to himself 'Do I want to be honest but broke, or do I want to prostitute myself and be loaded?'" With these stark sentences, he verbalized a dilemma that had been taking shape for years in the worlds of industrial and graphic design, but that had never been expressed so bluntly by speakers or participants at the IDCA – even if it was constantly on their minds.[2]

Through an examination of the papers and proceedings of the IDCA, which was the most prominent post-World War II forum in the United States and Europe for the discussion of pressing issues of concern to professional designers, I want in the following paragraphs to explore the position of the graphic, industrial, and to a certain extent also architectural designer during the years between roughly 1950 and 1975, when the world was dangerously divided by the so-called Cold War, and when the economy of the United States expanded greatly through business with Europe – thanks to the Marshall Plan – and other parts of the world. Designers working for large companies active both nationally and internationally had to develop different means to navigate new political, economic, and social circumstances. As business people, they sought to profit from these unprecedented conditions, because newly available jobs allowed them to expand their offices and become financially secure. At the same time, designers in all fields thought of themselves first of all as artists whose work should be appreciated for its creative qualities and not for its commercial success in a world where large corporations were vying to control the marketplace. They often expressed their ambivalence, though occasionally in covert terms. (Of course graphic and industrial designers were not the only people in creative professions struggling with the demon of "selling out." For architects it was an equally urgent issue, and visual artists – for example, Ad Reinhardt – also spoke with great passion about this problem.[3])

Several important studies have been written about IDCA, an organization that met during the month of June each year from 1951 to 2004 and that at its highpoint during the 1970s and 80s attracted thousands of designers to the bucolic grounds of the Aspen Institute for Humanistic Studies. However, none of these studies have examined the debates that took place in the organization as a means of understanding the particular position occupied by the designer in the post-World War II era.[4]

"The world's problem is now ours, and unless we take the lead in solving it creatively, there will be no more problems to solve."

Dr. Harold A. Taylor

1.1
Walter Paepcke, Jacques
Viénot, French industrial
designer, and Will Burtin,
graphic designer and
conference chair, at the
1956 IDCA conference.
Photo: Ferenc Berko.
Burtin Archive, RIT
Graphic Design Archives.

IDCA was the brainchild of Walter Paepcke.(ill.1.1) A successful businessman in Chicago, Paepke was also an intellectual, friendly not only with other business people such as Marshall Field III, but also with scholars such as Robert M. Hutchins, the president of the University of Chicago, and the philosopher Mortimer Adler. Aspen, Colorado, may seem to have been an odd place for a conference developed by a Chicagoan but for Paepcke it made perfect sense. Shortly after the end of World War II, he and his wife Elizabeth had purchased a substantial amount of real estate in what was then a moribund silver-mining town that by the 1940s had a population of less than 1000.[5] Surrounded by the Rocky Mountains, Aspen was, the Paepckes realized, an ideal place for skiing, an activity that over the next few decades would shed its initial aura as a sport enjoyed only by social elites to become accessible to broad segments of society. The Paepckes founded the Aspen Skiing Corporation (ill.1.2), built a ski lift, and created the beginnings of what is now a major resort destination.[6] However, the Paepckes wanted the town to be more than a locale devoted to physical entertainment. They also wanted it to be a center of cultural activity and therefore established the Aspen Institute for Humanistic Studies, which would serve as an overarching agency to sponsor a music festival and act as a meeting place for leaders in government, business, and education. IDCA was organized under the auspices of the Aspen Institute and quickly attracted a large audience.

Not by accident did Paepcke develop the idea for a design conference. However, with a traditional German-American upbringing, he had grown up in a setting where modern design had no presence. In fact, this son of a lumber-company owner preferred German Romanticism until the 1930s when his wife, who had studied painting at the School of the Art Institute of Chicago, introduced him to modern art. She convinced Paepcke, who had transformed his father's firm into

1.2
Herbert Bayer, "Aspen, Colorado, 1951–52," brochure advertising Aspen as a tourist destination for winter sports. Private collection.

a cardboard-box company called the Container Corporation of America (CCA), to hire modern artists to create the graphic identity of his business. Beginning in the mid-1930s, A. M. Cassandre, Jean Carlu, and Jean Hélion, among many others, were hired to participate in advertising campaigns not only to promote the use of cardboard boxes made by CCA, but also to establish the company as a modern, cultured operation. And indeed, the CCA's advertising campaigns utilizing the work of modern artists put the company on the map as a business that was willing to do things in a new way.(ill.1.3) Published from the mid-1930s onward in such magazines as *Fortune* and *Time*, the early advertisements made CCA's logo and name part of the ad. Over the years, that identifying information became less and less evident, and in the postwar series, "Great Ideas of Western Man" (inspired by the University of Chicago's "Great Books of the Western World" seminars), the company's name and logo were placed completely outside the artistic image. Today, the series as a whole still comes across with extraordinary power, which is reinforced by insightful quotations (often about civic duties) that the artists were asked to include. For example, the graphic designer Paul Rand was given a text by the Greek historian Herodotus about freedom of discussion.[7] Rand augmented the text with a silhouette of an Ionic column, which reveals the sculpted face of Herodotus seemingly emerging from the shadow of time.(ill.1.4) Nothing in the ad refers to cardboard or boxes, except for the company's name and logo at the bottom of the page. Paepcke understood early on that the branding of his business was more important than a specific message about the products it manufactured. Readers recognized the ads as creations of CCA and even if they did not read the text, they would remember the company's name in association with its high standard of design.[8]

The success of these advertising campaigns made Paepcke into a true believer in the power of modern art and a strong supporter of

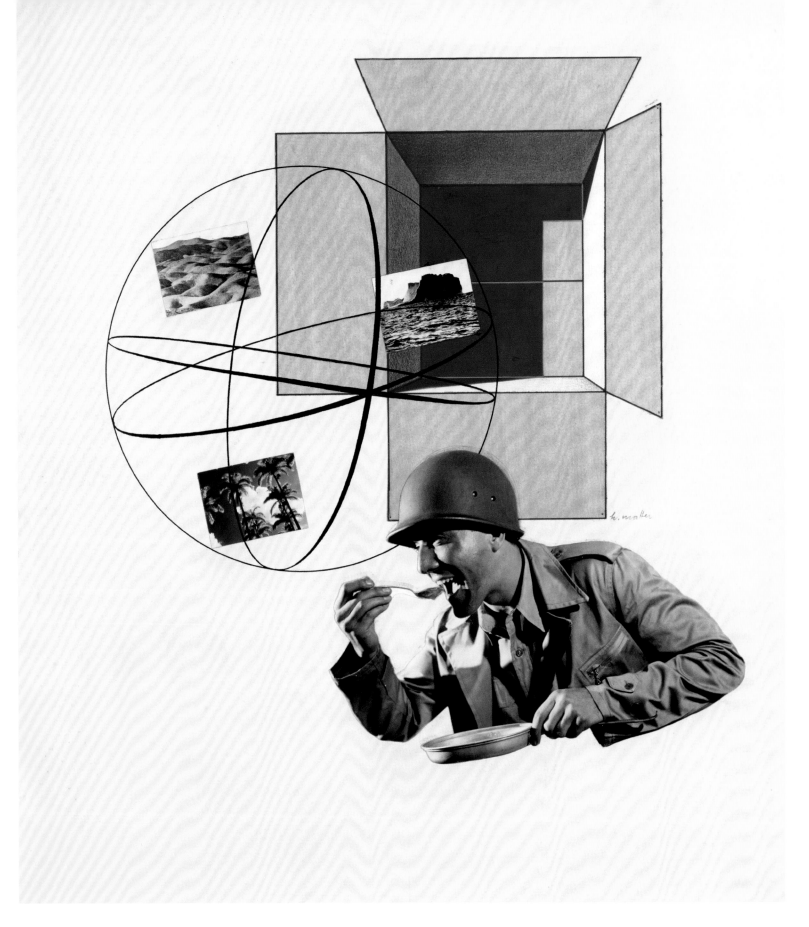

Great Ideas of Western Man: one of a series

Herodotus *on freedom of discussion*

It is impossible, if no more than one opinion is uttered, to make choice of the best: a man is forced then to follow whatever advice may have been given him; but if opposite speeches are delivered, then choice can be exercised. In like manner pure gold is not recognized by itself; but when we test it along with baser ore, we perceive which is the better.

Container Corporation of America

Aspen Institute
for Humanistic Studies

HOTEL JEROME

ASPEN | COLO.

CLOSE COVER BEFORE STRIKING

1.5
Herbert Bayer, matchbook
for Hotel Jerome and
the Aspen Institute, early
1950s.
Private collection.

healthy relationships between modern art and business. In the mid-1930s, he was actively involved in bringing the artist, designer, and former Bauhaus teacher László Moholy-Nagy to Chicago and in the founding of the New Bauhaus in that city. After the war, he hired another former Bauhaus student and teacher, Herbert Bayer, to work for him as a design consultant in Aspen. Paepcke, who seems to have liked gathering high-profile, creative people around him, asked Bayer to help in the restoration of his properties in Aspen, and to give the town, and all the activities being planned to take place there, a unifying graphic identity. Bayer designed not only the brochures that advertised Aspen as a ski destination, but also the graphics for the Hotel Jerome, which was by then also part of Paepcke's growing "empire," and for the events that took place under the auspices of the Aspen Institute. Thus, through Bayer, there was a direct connection between Aspen and the pre-war Bauhaus in Germany. This did not mean, however, that the town's graphic identity was inspired by a characteristic Bauhaus use of abstract forms. Instead, Bayer chose the aspen leaf as the identifier for everything relating to the town. For the Aspen Institute he embellished the leaf with a silhouette of a man with raised arm (looking not unlike Le Corbusier's Modulor man, Bayer's was probably a reference to classical antiquity as a source for the humanities in general); and materials for the Hotel Jerome showed a leaf with the hotel's name and a large letter "J" inside or next to it (ill.1.5). An image of the aspen leaf would also be applied to the earliest, Bayer-designed graphic materials printed to announce the annual design conferences.

If Bayer was a link between Aspen and the Bauhaus, the International Design Conferences definitely brought the Bauhaus – a pioneering institution in the realm of art intersecting with commerce – to that town, not as a formal teaching facility, but as a think tank where participants could discuss ideas about promoting design as a source of mass production by industry. Together with Bayer and Egbert Jacobson, art director at the Chicago office of the Container Corporation of America, Paepcke developed the concept for an annual conference in the serene surroundings of Aspen, where designers would meet with executives and top managers of corporations to improve mutual understanding and find ways to enhance their collaboration. The goal was to convince the businessmen that designers should participate in the decision-making process at the management level. The first conference (in 1951) therefore took as its theme "Design as a Function of Management."[9]

Creating a better understanding between designers and business managers may have seemed at the time like an uphill battle. Paepcke, however, had already seen the benefits of good design and realized that the post-World War II corporate world in general needed the creative assistance of modern designers. Corporations had become increasingly prominent in the American business world since the mid-nineteenth century. They had been created, on the one hand, through horizontal mergers of related companies (production, distribution, finance, etc.) to strengthen control over the market and, on the other hand, through the establishment of a vertical bureaucratic hierarchy of executives and managers that, when operating in a unified way, could oversee all aspects of the business. While corporations emerged as critical players in the American capitalist system, many people resented their existence, especially in the 1920s and 30s when they were often described as soulless entities that used their power to create totally efficient organizations in which thousands of people labored, largely without personal interrelationship.[10]

This hostility changed to some degree after World War II, when the incorporation of American industry was more or less accepted as a *fait accompli* and people were willing to give credit to American companies for the vital contributions they had made to the war effort. In addition, a huge appetite had developed for American-made consumer goods, many of which had not been available for years because the materials from which they were made had been pre-empted by the war. As their desires for such goods were increasingly satisfied, people became more willing to regard big businesses as important contributors to a healthy economy.[11] Moreover, the world in which corporations were operating had changed considerably. With the beginning of the Cold War, the US had become one of the world's two superpowers and initiated an effort to gain economic and political control over the western hemisphere, for example through the Marshall Plan, which enabled the United States to restore European economies and create huge markets abroad for mass-produced American commodities. In such a vastly expanded consumer market, competition was stronger than it had been before the war.[12] Traditional means of standing out through quality of product and low prices were no longer effective. American manufacturers therefore embraced a new strategy that would enable consumers anywhere in the world to visually recognize their products through design and through the creation of unique brand identities.

Walter Paepcke was very much aware of these developments and pointed them out in a lecture to Yale alumni in Chicago in 1950 or early 1951 when he declared:

> American business faces a new era and a new phase of competition. Because of the leveling or equalizing processes now generally practiced throughout industry (automatic machinery, uniform wage and marketing practices) the opportunities for effective competition based on traditional factors of price and quality of product have been greatly diminished. Competition of the present and future must be based on new factors, on the appearance, attractiveness and appeal of the product, and on the reputation of the companies who make and sell it.[13]

Design thus emerged as the means by which industrialists would be able to distinguish their companies. They needed graphic designers capable of creating unique logos that on the one hand would be recognizable worldwide, and, on the other hand, would be legible in all formats in which they would be used: on a very small business card, on a letterhead or annual report, and also on the scale of a large neon sign on top of a high-rise building. The graphic designers responsible for the two-dimensional representation of the corporation would have to relate closely to the industrial designers who shaped the look of the products manufactured by the company, and vice versa. Perhaps the most effective example of such interconnectivity is the role played by architect and designer Eliot Noyes, who after World War II was brought into the powerful office-machine company IBM by his friend Thomas Watson, Jr., who had assumed leadership of the company from his father. As part of an overall reorganization, Noyes was asked to provide a master plan for the total physical appearance of the company – its offices, products, and graphic imagery. For the architectural and interior work Noyes brought in top designers of the period, such as Marcel Breuer, Paul Rudolph, and Eero Saarinen; for the two-dimensional design he told the company to hire Paul Rand. It was Rand who created the company's muscular logo and chose the color palette used for such products as the famous Selectric typewriter designed by Noyes himself.[14] (ills. 1.6 and 1.7)

Not all corporations had as strong a design sense as IBM and certainly not all corporate leaders felt sufficiently comfortable with giving designers as much control as IBM did. Many other businesses preferred to empower inside managers and therefore set up their own corporate offices devoted to market research.[15] However, such internal organizational controls created significant obstacles for designers who felt that their artistic faculties were compromised by the input of marketing managers.[16] Such conflicting attitudes toward design took a huge toll on designers' self-image. IDCA records reveal how that self-image, as well as designers' thinking about their role vis-à-vis their employers and clients, changed over time. While IDCA was not a single-issue think tank, the organization does enable us to study a number of pressing topics in the design world by following their trajectories through multiple years of conference discourse. In this sense, IDCA is clearly an important touchstone for understanding the challenges that helped to shape modern design during the mid- and late twentieth century.

1.6
Eliot Noyes, IBM Selectric Typewriter, 1961.
Molded aluminum.
Photo: Bertrand Prévost.
Musée National d'Art Moderne, Paris. Courtesy of International Business Machines Corporation,
© 1961 International Business Machines Corporation.

1.7
Paul Rand, IBM product
colors, n.d.

"A Design Department, properly staffed and given support and wide latitude, can enhance a company's reputation as an alert and progressive business institution within and without its organization, and assist materially in improving its competitive position."

Walter Paepcke

1.8 overleaf
Marcello Nizzoli, Lettera
22 Portable Typewriter
for Olivetti, 1950.
Enameled metal
San Francisco Museum
of Modern Art, Gift of
Dung Ngo.

Approaching the 54-year history of IDCA, one can distinguish several periods. These are, roughly, 1951–61, when all conferences were devoted to design and the corporate world; 1962–72, when the conference topics reveal growing concern with social, political, and environmental changes and with how best to respond to these; 1973–90, when the themes were more theoretical, dealing with issues of interest to designers, but were not necessarily directly concerned with design itself; and 1991–2004, the final years in which IDCA found it increasingly difficult to stay financially afloat while still maintaining the high quality of previous conferences. The remainder of this essay focuses on the first two periods and on the designers' struggles to determine their position as citizens who were sensitive to the changes of their time and who did not want to be accused of selling out to commerce.

Walter Paepcke's major goal for the conferences was from the beginning a straightforward one: that is, to improve the relationship between business and design. He especially wanted to ensure that business people and designers would learn to understand one another, and that designers would have a say in business on the same level as that of management. Everyone involved in the organization of the first conference was aware of this goal. Indeed, the reports of the planning committee (consisting of such luminaries as Frank Stanton, the president of CBS, Stanley Marcus, president of Neiman Marcus, and Leo Lionni, art director of *Fortune* magazine, in addition to Paepcke's representatives Herbert Bayer and Egbert Jacobson) spoke consistently of "integrated design," and the preliminary plan for the sessions was organized around this concept.[17] When in the spring of 1951 the printed announcement of the conference went out, the organizers included a manifesto-like statement composed by Paepcke, in which he wrote:

Design in this sense is the concern of all management, the officers and directors, the sales, advertising and production executives. Through the appearance and planning of its offices and factory work spaces, the influence of the designer and his consultants penetrates the entire organization, contributing to more efficient and congenial working conditions and to better employee morale.

A Design Department, properly staffed and given support and wide latitude, can enhance a company's reputation as an alert and progressive business institution within and without its organization, and assist materially in improving its competitive position.[18]

The designers on the organizing committee must have embraced this testimonial, but they worried about how to get business people to pay attention and get involved. In its report of March 27 the group stated, "It was the consensus that in order to interest management, the program should be directly related to design as an important element of modern business; to its special applications, its personnel and their training, to its value in manufacture, sales, distribution and public relations and its final dependence on management for successful realization."[19] Apparently, this acknowledgement of business interests did the trick: the management side was well represented in "Design as a Function of Management." Of course we may assume that those business people who did attend had already more or less converted to Paepcke's vision. In particular, those who spoke in the sessions (including Andrew McNally III of Rand McNally & Co., and Burton G. Tremaine of The Miller Company) were probably friendly with Paepcke, who may well have known what they were likely to say. But there were also representatives of many other corporations, including General Electric, S. C. Johnson & Son, Inc., Eli Lilly & Co., and the Olivetti Corporation of America, in attendance and presumably willing to listen to the arguments being presented.

Of all these companies, the Italian Olivetti company was especially respected by post-World War II designers because of its attention to design in all fields, from its architecture to its products to its posters and advertisements. Founded in 1908 in Ivrea, Italy, by Camillo Olivetti as a producer of typewriters and other office machinery, the company became known worldwide after World War II when Camillo's son, Adriano, took over. Having spent several years during the fascist era in the United States and England studying the industries of those countries, Adriano developed the idea that part of the profits of his company should be returned to the community. Bringing in respected designers to plan new buildings for Olivetti factories and workers' housing, to create new appearances for the office machines produced by the company, and to redesign its publicity was part of this concept. One of the great designers hired by Adriano Olivetti was Marcello Nizzoli, whose award-winning, portable Lettera 22 typewriter (1950, ill. 1.8) became a must-have for many writers because of its relatively light weight and its compact look due to the smoothly shaped wrapping around the internal mechanisms. The organizers of the first IDCA conference were well aware of design-world interest in Olivetti machinery. With the support

of Leo Lionni (who, in addition to being art director of *Fortune* magazine, also did graphic design work for Olivetti, ill. 1.9), several Olivetti products were on display at the conference.[20]

By all accounts, the first IDCA conference was a great success, creating a model that organizers would wish to follow in subsequent years. Thus, the conferences of 1952 and 1953 were again organized by Paepcke and his associates, under the same theme, "Design as a Function of Management." The 1952 conference seems to have been smaller than the others. Listings in the various IDCA archives and in Reyner Banham's 1974 collection of papers delivered at Aspen indicate that there were only four speakers at this conference, two designers and two businessmen: the architect and inventor Richard Buckminster Fuller; Richard B. Gump, president of Gump's Inc.; Alfred A. Knopf, a publisher; and Walter D. Teague, industrial designer and president of the Society of Industrial Designers.[21] It was Teague who, drawing from experience, spoke most directly about the designer's role vis-à-vis both the consumer and business management. Having worked as an industrial designer for many major companies, including Boeing, Con Edison, DuPont, and Eastman Kodak, he advised his audience to be aware of what the company that hired them could deliver as far as manufacturing techniques, efficiency of operations, and the abilities of the staff in general were concerned. He added: "Industrial design . . . should avoid the tendency to freeze forms resulting in dangerous and unavoidable clichés. It should also understand and solve the necessary restrictions placed upon it by the manufacturer's plant operation, tools, the necessary co-operation between designer and engineer, without which work does not progress, and ultimately the price level."[22] In a subtle way, Teague warned IDCA participants that work for the corporate world was not going to be as easy as the pleasant gathering of all parties on the meadows in Aspen appeared to suggest.

After the third annual meeting in 1953, Paepcke announced that he would no longer be responsible for the organization of the conferences and that the designers, if they wanted to continue to convene, should take over the organization.[23] The archival records do not reveal if his decision came as a surprise to anyone, but it is understandable in view of the fact that the conferences had been a drain not only on Paepcke's personal finances, but also on his business, as several of his employees had worked throughout the prior three years to organize the conferences. Paepcke may also have realized that he could not

continue to count on his friends in the business world to attend these conferences. They had probably already conveyed the ideas they wished to offer. If the conferences were to continue, others would have to take care of the invitations. Faced with this challenge, the designers chose to continue the annual meetings, formally organizing themselves as the International Design Conference in Aspen (incorporated in the State of Illinois on October 22, 1954, with R. Hunter Middleton, director of typeface design at the Ludlow Typograph Company in Chicago, as its chair).[24]

The relationship with corporate America was not discussed at all in the next two conferences ("Planning: The Basis of Design," 1954, and "Crossroads: What Are the Directions of the Arts," 1955). Clearly, the organizers wanted to show that they were now working on their own and turned instead to the other question that constituted an ongoing theme during the first 25 years of IDCA, namely, what is the designers' role in society; how could they better understand man's needs and aspirations, or how could they arrive at a "better understanding of design as an instrument of social progress."[25]

This line of investigation changed radically again in the 1956 conference, which had as its overall theme "Ideas on the Future of Man and Design".(ill.1.10) Chaired by graphic designer Will Burtin, the conference's first session returned to the original idea of "Management and Design," a relationship about which by the mid-1950s many designers were less optimistic than they had been earlier in the decade. Burtin commented in his opening speech that there were not as many business managers present as one might have expected for a conference with this sub-theme, but he wondered if that wasn't actually a good thing, for "it does not make sense to gloss over the evidences of design having become in many cases servile to business and sales curves to such a degree that the most serious consequences to moral standards have developed."[26] In the wake of Teague's earlier warning in 1952, this is the first time that we find an expression of genuine concern about what designers were doing to themselves by working closely with corporations. "Servility to business and sales curves" was only one of multiple ways to express what had begun to bother the designers. By 1956, it was clear to them that their cooperation with management (something that had seemed so important only five years earlier) had a downside when it involved managers who might be knowledgeable about production and distribution, but who lacked the requisite experience to judge modern design. Yet, it was the responsibility of

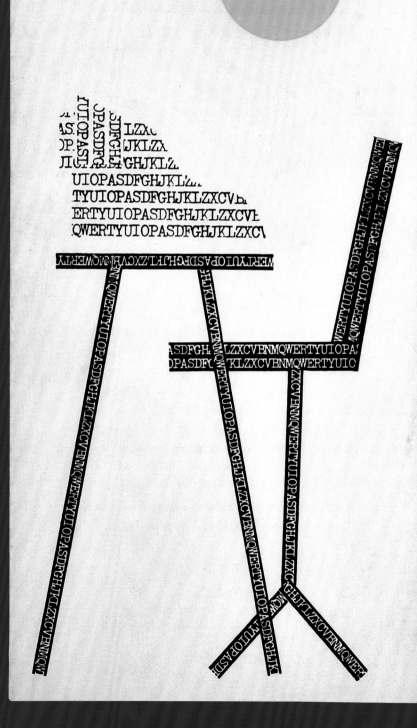

1.9
Leo Lionni, flyer advertising
Olivetti "Lexikon 80"
Typewriter, n.d.
Lionni Archive, RIT Graphic
Design Archives.

1.10
Speakers on the stage in the big tent, IDCA 1956. Panel: Professions of Design. Speakers from left to right: Saul Bass, Sori Yanagi, interpreter, F. H. K. Henrion, James Fitch, Alberto Rosselli, Max Frisch, Will Burtin, Joseph Mueller-Brockmann, and Garrett Eckbo.
Photo by Ferenc Berko. Burtin Archive, RIT Graphic Design Archives.

precisely those managers to analyse market research and, often on that basis alone, determine the saleability of a given product. Instead of inspiring business executives to produce functional objects that were shaped by an aesthetic expertise, designers feared that the reigning system led to the production only of undistinguished objects that a manager's untrained eye could appreciate. J. Gordon Lippincott, a product designer with Lippincott & Margulies, related to his fellow conferees: "Thus, rather than having a design-oriented management, we dealt in the main with management-oriented design."[27] Indeed, words like "gimmicks" and "sales gadgets" could be heard regularly in IDCA discussions. The British designer Misha Black, known for his exhibits at the 1951 Festival of Britain, pointed out in his IDCA lecture of 1956,

> A high design standard can only be achieved when at least one director at the top level of management really believes in design, has the visual perception to distinguish the good from the meretricious, and cares as a human being that the goods which his factory produces or the physical manifestation of the services he controls should please the senses of sight and touch while satisfying those emotions which react to efficiency and fitness for purpose.[28]

Needless to say, Black knew of too many companies where such a leader was missing.

In addition to unhappiness about marketing issues and the general lack of understanding or appreciation they perceived in their dealings with management, designers were deeply unsettled by yet another issue: planned obsolescence, which in design terms meant that one was supposed to create something that within a few years would be out of fashion and in need of replacement. Such an approach ran directly counter to the ethical thinking of professional designers, whose self-image was the result of training that in essence dated back to a pre-industrial era in which craftsmen produced what amounted to art objects based on a specific need, rather than items generated by commercial considerations of how many could be sold. When the concept of planned obsolescence first emerged, a few designers tried to justify this approach to production and consumer purchase by declaring it to be a characteristically American phenomenon and genuinely modern. J. Gordon Lippincott, for example, wrote in 1947 in his book *Design for Business*:

1.11
Craig Ellwood and Eliot
Noyes on stage in the
big tent, IDCA, 1960.
Photo by Ferenc Berko.
IDCA Archives.

The American consumer *expects* new and better products every year . . . His acceptance of change toward better living is indeed the American's greatest asset . . . Our custom of trading in our automobiles every year, of having a new refrigerator, vacuum cleaner or electric iron every three or four years is economically sound. Our willingness to part with something *before* it is completely worn out is . . . truly an American habit, and it is soundly based on our economy of abundance.[29]

Such a supposedly patriotic defense of planned obsolescence was difficult to sustain among designers, even though in essence it meant that their offices would regularly receive commissions to rethink their designs and, with minimal changes in color and materials, make them look new and different again. For a creative person of the 1950s and 60s, who believed that a beautiful form resulted from a thorough understanding of the function of an object, such an approach to industrial production of their designs was unacceptable.

Designers' problems with the corporate world were not static over time. While in the booming economy of the 1950s the corporation was considered to be an intrusive nuisance that pretended to have knowledge of something – design – about which it often knew nothing, by the 1960s when the race to the moon, the arms race, and the generally close relationship between America's military and its industrial sector required that employees accept the country's political ambitions and conform, the view of the corporation as a soulless and parasitic organism resurfaced. IDCA was of course affected by this change in attitude, which very soon emerged in its debates. For the tenth anniversary of the Aspen conferences in 1960, a decision was made to return to the organization's earliest theme, "The Corporation and the Designer". (ill.1.11) The chair of this particular conference was George D. Culler, director of the San Francisco Museum of Art (now SFMOMA).[30] Culler's initial written statements, dating from November 1959, indicate that he had a rather straightforward idea in mind for what the conference would be about. He believed that of the three interacting parties – the designer, the corporation, and the client – the corporation or manufacturer was least understood. Culler therefore proposed to present a number of case studies in which representatives of corporations would describe their working methods, especially with regard to design, after which a number of panelists would ask questions.[31] The board presumably endorsed this format. However, when one reads the introductory remarks by Culler at the opening of the conference, it becomes clear that there must have been a major change. Instead of talking about how fuller knowledge of the inner workings of a corporation could assist the designer in achieving the best results for the execution and marketing of his products, Culler spoke about large corporations and their "resistance to change," and wondered how a creative individual could be innovative in such a context.[32] And he was not alone in posing this question. Paul Fine, vice president for the Center for Research in Marketing, Inc., for example, made the point that there is "very little room for creativity within the organization" of a corporation. And even the British businessman Leslie Julius, who together with his wife, Rosamind, turned her family's business, the Hille furniture company, into an unusually successful mid-size producer of modern furniture – especially after they brought in the designer Robin Day – told his audience, "As a result of the concentration of power into larger and larger units there is less room for the intuitive manager and for the individualist."[33]

Analogous thinking on the part of the various presenters cannot have come about by accident. On the contrary, we must assume that these speakers had either read or heard about some recent books that had had a huge impact on people's thinking about the world of business, especially William H. Whyte's bestseller *The Organization Man*. Its thesis argues that large organizations, whether corporations or governments or even universities, require their employees to accept a certain code of behavior, which Whyte called the Social Ethic. This ethic "rationalizes the organization's demands for fealty and gives those who offer it wholeheartedly a sense of dedication in doing so – *in extremis*, you might say, it converts what would seem in other times a bill of no rights into a restatement of individualism."[34] Workers in these organizations had been socially engineered to become individuals who wanted to belong, who wanted to be part of a group of co-workers all of whom lived in similar suburban settings. We clearly see here the beginnings of what came to be associated with "the sixties," a period marked by skepticism of 1950s conformism in which many of the principal institutions and organizations that had contributed to the postwar economic boom came under scrutiny. Designers of course felt compelled to participate in this reconsideration of the conditions that had made so many of them successful, but that at the same time seemed to undermine their creativity.

In IDCA conferences of the following years, the political and social unrest caused by the Cold War and counterculture came increasingly to the fore. As mentioned previously, many speakers at the 1961 conference expressed fears about what could happen when two superpowers escalated their respective military build-ups in an apparent competition to control the entire world and even the universe. In 1962, when the conference was devoted to "the Environment," the chair, Ralph Eckerstrom, stated in his opening remarks, "I believe that we do not overstate the case when we say that the problem of Environment is second only in importance today to the problem of avoiding a nuclear holocaust. After the question of continuing life itself on the planet, comes the question of how Man is to live his life."[35] These now read as strikingly prescient remarks, but it was the following year's conference that was most clearly influenced by the Cold War and America's role in it. Devoted to "Design and the American Image Abroad" and organized by the architecture critic and editor of *Architectural Form*, Peter Blake, who was associated with the United States Information Agency, the conference focused attention on the impact of films and other sources of propaganda that the US sent abroad, especially to countries behind the Iron Curtain. According to Reyner Banham (ill.1.12), the conference failed because too many participants had attended in order to "grind political axes".[36] These interactions led Banham to ponder in a lengthy if humorous summary statement delivered at the end of the 1964 conference ("Directions and Dilemmas" chaired by Eliot Noyes) how much IDCA had moved away from its original aims, and how much the designers' ethical position with respect to their clients and their clients' customers had changed: "[W]e are no longer dealing with a confrontation between management and design, but between designers and the problems of the world at large." And, Banham added,

> It is clear from the many pieces of paper that have been submitted to me that a lot of people among the conferees are more aware of this change than we may have been up here on the platform. They came expecting the Aspen of tradition and were surprised, even delighted, to find a different Aspen, an IDCA prepared to march on Washington, to applaud a sit-in as triumph of design.[37]

The trajectory of this engaged attitude came to a halt in 1970 when counterculture made its way into the conference in the shape of free-speech-movement-inspired Berkeley architecture students and representatives of the San Francisco architects' collaborative, Ant Farm. And then there were the specially invited French philosophers and designers, who had already experienced the student revolt of May 1968 in Paris, and who branded the American designers gathered in the beautiful Aspen setting as representatives of the establishment who refused to see that problems of design and environment were ideological problems produced by a capitalist society. The conferees were shocked to the core by their experience of being identified with the kind of people who, as artists, they had always tried hard to avoid becoming. The conference barely survived.[38]

Meeting with fellow board members at the end of the 1970 conference, IDCA president Eliot Noyes proposed that the organization and its conferences should be terminated. In his opinion, the Aspen conferences had run their course. The board decided not to follow Noyes' advice, and he consequently stepped down as president (ill.1.13). Banham must have been in agreement with Noyes, as suggested by his expressions of frustration in both the introduction and epilogue of his *Aspen Papers* book, the whole of which is consequently drenched in melancholy for the wonderful meetings of the 1950s and 60s. But the architecture and design historian laid out his thoughts about the issues that drove IDCA debates most clearly in an unpublished memoir found among his papers at the Getty Research Institute:

> Increasingly, throughout the Sixties, the old principle of guilt-by-association accused the design-profession of complicity in a corrupt society equal to that of commercial evil until finally the activists' resolutions of 1970 called upon IDCA to vote commercial design out of existence, and thus to withdraw the very foundations on which the Conferences had been based at their beginning in 1951.[39]

Indeed, after 1970, the conference organizers seemingly did not want to discuss design. The conferences entered a new and different phase, with themes and presentations ("Paradox," 1971, and "Performance," 1973, for example) that were much broader than those of preceding years and that at first glance seemed to have little to do with design. Nevertheless, in terms of numbers of participants, the conferences of the 1970s and 80s were the most successful in the entire 54-year history of gatherings in Aspen.

"The American consumer expects new and better products every year . . . His acceptance of change toward better living is indeed the American's greatest asset . . . Our willingness to part with something before it is completely worn out is . . . truly an American habit, and it is soundly based on our economy of abundance."

J. Gordon Lippincott

1.12
Herbert Bayer and Reyner
Banham on stage in the
big tent, IDCA, 1963.
Photo by Ferenc Berko.
IDCA Archives.

This success came to an end after the 1990 "Growing by Design" conference, a very expensive meeting accompanied by amusement rides and other unusual features about children and their play that put IDCA in significant debt. As a result, the organization entered an inexorable downward spiral. With the exception of a few successful conferences, including "Gestalt: Visions of German Design" (1996) and "SportsDesign: It's not about Sports, It's about Design" (1998), the conferences had to be simplified and, through themes such as "Bare Bones: Making More with Less" (1991), emphasized the precariousness of the situation. But IDCA's problem was not only financial; it also had to do with the age of the organization. After more than 40 years, the conference had become too identified with the highly respected generation of mid-century modern designers such as Saul Bass or Ivan

Chermayeff. It was difficult for younger professionals to break into the leadership circle, which meant that they began to look elsewhere. Other, trendier attractions drew their attention, especially the TED (Technology Entertainment Design) conferences, which had been established in 1984 by former IDCA board member Richard S. Wurman and whose popularity began to take off in the 1990s. It was the combination of design and technology that gave the TED conferences their innovative character; their short (18-minute) and therefore necessarily pointed presentations also helped establish TED's status as the new place to be.

Yet, the most important reason for IDCA's decline may well have been that the relationship between design and commerce had changed dramatically since the organization was founded four decades earlier. By the 1990s, corporate design involved much more than shaping a

1.13
Still from "IDCA 70", a film
by Eli Noyes and Claudia
Weill, showing Eliot Noyes
as the only board member
raising his hand in favor in a
vote regarding the question
of whether IDCA should
be discontinued. All other
members voted against.

company's identity or aesthetically modeling its products. Collaborative possibilities of design and the corporate world are now more challenging and more complex. Indeed "design thinking" is a concept that today applies to domains whose boundaries far exceed those envisioned in the postwar years. Designers now help businesses to rethink their entire organizational structures, and they themselves have become entrepreneurs. While there may always be design firms such as Pentagram and Landor Associates that specialize in the branding of corporations, today product design has become synonymous with innovation through technology and with start-up companies. Design firms have become worth investing in and are thus "a core ingredient" for venture capitalism. The Paepckes or Olivettis, who considered it to be their responsibility to give back to the community through quality design by first-class designers, have now been replaced by designers themselves, who with the help of modern technology and the support of wealthy investors are able to reach worldwide audiences.[40]

The fear of selling out to commerce will always exist amongst those who are active in artistic fields. At the same time, however, designers have finally attained the corporate positions to which their predecessors of the 1950s and 60s aspired. Today's designers are an integral part of the management of a company or, even better, they run the company themselves. From their perch at the apex of the corporate world, designers interact directly with boards and shareholders. They no longer need an organization such as IDCA.

ESTABLISHMENT MODERNISM & ITS DISCONTENTS IDCA IN THE 'LONG SIXTIES'

GREG CASTILLO

Two annual sessions of the International Design Conference in Aspen (IDCA) erupted in controversy as participants confronted the profession's collusion with Cold War-era government and industry. The 1963 IDCA, "Design and the American Image Abroad," showcased efforts by the United States Information Agency (USIA) to shape foreign perceptions of America. These branding efforts had remained unseen within the US due to a provision of the 1948 Smith-Mundt Act, a Congressional bill that allotted federal funds for foreign propaganda campaigns with the proviso that they were not to be redirected toward US audiences. The consumer affluence intrinsic to an "American Way of Life," promoted globally as "People's Capitalism" by the USIA, came under attack at a subsequent Aspen gathering. School buses laden with self-designated "ecofreaks" from Berkeley and San Francisco turned "Environment by Design," the 1970 IDCA, into a call to arms. Rather than attempting to fully chronicle these IDCA conferences, this essay explores the cultural and political contexts of both events: for 1963, the development of design practices promoting an American Way of Life to audiences within the US sphere of influence and behind the Iron Curtain; and for 1970, the counterculture ethos of the outlaw and its celebration of environmental pacifism.

Design and the American Image Abroad, IDCA 1963

Publicists promoted the 1963 IDCA as a unique "opportunity to evaluate visual communications designed specifically to shape the American image abroad. Not previously available to the public, this material will include motion pictures, television films, exhibits and visual journalism."[1] Conferees reacted with disdain. According to a local reporter, "Of all the designers and other participants we talked to during and after the recent design conference not one expressed pleasure with the program he had paid to attend. Nor can we blame them . . . It is one thing to watch and hear of demonstrations of propaganda techniques, it is another to be subjected to propaganda at the same time."[2] The newspaper article reiterated a long-standing theme of conservative hostility to overseas "public diplomacy" – a term preferred by USIA staff, for obvious reasons. The infamous Congressional hearings led by Senator Joseph McCarthy, which decried the presence of "socialists, misfits, and perverts" within the US State Department, had excoriated federal overseas information programs. In April 1953 McCarthy's aides, Roy Cohn and David Schine, descended upon libraries at US information centers across Western Europe on a "clean-up expedition." Asserting the discovery of 30,000

subversive volumes by "some seventy-five different communist authors," they left chaos in their wake. Librarians quit or were dismissed; books were removed and in some cases burned.[3] McCarthyism's transatlantic escapade degraded one of America's most strategic cultural assets: the carefully nurtured perception that intellectual freedom buttressed US democracy. A decade later, according to the official IDCA chronicler, the architectural historian and critic Reyner Banham, Aspen participants witnessed a provincial re-enactment of McCarthy's European adventure: "The week began with systematic microphone-hogging by right wing elements (in genuine tennis shoes, yet!), progressed by way of a complete change of the Washington personnel present – from 'observers' to, frankly, spies – and finished with an attempt by one of the Senate committees to impound the tapes and transcripts!"[4]

Perhaps resulting from alarms sounded in Washington, documentation of the 1963 IDCA proceedings remains fragmentary. However, their focus of interest – namely USIA efforts to devise a compelling brand for America in order to promote its overseas interests – can be examined in detail through abundant archival records.

The Eisenhower administration created the USIA in 1953 in large part as a means of insulating the State Department from McCarthy's witch-hunt. Having seen firsthand the carnage caused by conventional weaponry, Eisenhower regarded psychological warfare as a humane alternative. "Psychological activity is not a field of endeavor separable from the main body of diplomatic, economic, and military measures by which the United States seeks to achieve its national objectives. It is an ingredient of such measures," declared presidential advisor C. D. Jackson, the former chief of the Political Warfare Division of Allied forces in northwest Europe.[5] When John Foster Dulles, Eisenhower's incoming Secretary of State, renounced all authority over politically vulnerable overseas propaganda programs, the president created the USIA as a clearing house for federally funded publications, broadcasts, films, and exhibitions promoting America abroad. Swayed by McCarthy, Congress immediately slashed the USIA personnel budget by one third. By 1960, the grand total for all federal information ventures was $300 million, or a mere 0.6 per cent of the $50 billion allocated for national security. Two years later, when USIA director Edward R. Murrow presented the agency's budget to the House of Representatives, a hostile congressman asked the veteran broadcaster how many homosexuals he had cut from payroll in the past year.[6] Long after McCarthy's demise, meager funding and ill repute still bedeviled USIA operations.

"Psychological activity is not a field of endeavor separable from the main body of diplomatic, economic, and military measures by which the United States seeks to achieve its national objectives. It is an ingredient of such measures."

Presidential advisor C. D. Jackson

The agency's publications earned a drubbing from critics at the 1963 IDCA. Invited speaker Patwant Singh, the founding editor of *Design*, a New Delhi-based journal, disparaged USIA publishing efforts in India. He called *SPAN*, a *Life* magazine knockoff, "dismal in typography, layouts, page make-up, and . . . paper stock." In contrast, Singh proclaimed *Ameryka* (ill.2.1), the Polish translation of the USIA monthly, *America Illustrated*, "a highly professional job."[7] These differences in production quality disclosed structural disparities within the agency. USIA budgets reflected agency priorities, with European operations attracting the lion's share of staff and resources. Programs relied on the initiative of an embassy-based staff organized into "country teams" that generated a "country plan" for their territory. Four area directors coordinated activities within global regions and with USIA headquarters in Washington, which provided the appropriate publicity materials or

funds to produce them in the field.[8] By 1963, the publication division had printed 12 million brochures, five million books, and 86 magazines and newspapers in 25 languages (ill.2.2).[9]

Despite the impressive production figures, USIA publications failed to project a suitable American image, according to critics at Aspen. Assessments of output ranged from "dull and impersonal" to "too opulent" for target audiences.[10] "The designer should understand . . . the advantages Soviet publications abroad enjoy by 'looking poor' and indigenous, rather than obviously imported and well-heeled as do American magazines," asserted Thomas W. Braden, a conference panelist identified on the IDCA program as the owner of the Oceanside *Blade-Tribune* – raising the question of how a small-town newspaper publisher had acquired his expertise on Soviet propaganda. The answer lay in Braden's previous job as a CIA operative in charge of covert

activities in Western Europe, where he lubricated local media with clandestine cash incentives to generate positive coverage of the US. None of this was known to IDCA participants – the dark op was blown only in 1967 by an exposé in the New Left journal *Ramparts*.[11] Braden's invitation to speak at Aspen suggests that much more went into IDCA event planning than was apparent to the casual conference goer.

USIA film and television production received more positive reviews from audiences at the 1963 IDCA.[12] In the previous year alone, the agency had issued 183 films, four fifths of them produced abroad, and 197 newsreels (ill.2.3). An additional off-the-books operation, code-named "Kingfish," used federal funds to subsidize commercial MGM newsreel production, providing favorable coverage of political events to dozens of Asian and African nations.[13] Former NBC producer Charles Hill managed USIA television, which supplied programming to broadcasters in 47 nations.[14] The USIA film division, administered by Hollywood insider George Stevens, Jr., engaged fresh directorial talent to forge a new propaganda genre that *Newsweek* dubbed the "soft policy" film.[15] Circulation of 50,000 USIA film prints reached an estimated audience of 600 million.[16] To assess differences in Western and Eastern Bloc filmmaking, IDCA participants viewed West and East German documentaries on the Berlin Wall: a piece of Iron Curtain infrastructure that USIA propagandists greeted with open arms. They sowed electrifying images of Berlin's division around the world in a traveling photographic exhibition and in films and television broadcasts, providing funds for the West German government to bring 750 foreign journalists to see the Wall for themselves.[17] Aspen audiences judged a Soviet Bloc documentary on the Wall, replete with hyperbolic narrative devices, much inferior to the "soft policy" alternative favored farther west.[18]

2.1

Published in Russian and Polish editions, *America Illustrated*, a monthly pictorial magazine published by the USIA, provided an optimistic view of the US that occasionally touched on the nation's conflicts, much to the displeasure of Congressional conservatives. Photos of urban riots in a 1964 issue on civil rights resulted in USIA staff being called to defend the agency's editorial practices before the Committee on Un-American Activities. US National Archives. Reproduced in Wilson P. Dizard, Jr., *Inventing Public Diplomacy: The Story of the USIA* (2004), p.124.

2.2

Closely associated with USIA publishing and press activities were a host of information outlets. US Information Centers located in city centers hosted lectures, discussion groups, English lessons, concerts and exhibits; bookmobiles, like this one shown in Burma in 1953, provided USIA publications to readers outside the urban core. National Archives. Published in Nicholas J. Cull, *The Cold War and the United States Information Agency: American Propaganda and Public Diplomacy, 1945–1989* (Cambridge: Cambridge University Press, 2009).

2.3
In a field adjoining a village fortified against Viet Cong incursions, Vietnamese villagers watch a USIA film in this 1963 *LIFE* magazine photograph by Michael Rougier. USIA documentary filmmaking achieved critical acclaim in the mid-1960s under the direction of George Stephens, Jr., and Edward R. Murrow, garnering multiple Oscar nominations and awards from international film festivals in Venice, Cannes, and Bilbao.
Michael Rougier/The LIFE Picture Collection/Getty Images.

2.4
Will Burtin, a German
émigré and former art
director for *Fortune*
magazine, specialized in
postwar exhibition design
promoting technological and
scientific innovation and its
public benefits for clients
ranging from chemical
and pharmaceutical
corporations to the federal
government. *Plastics
in America*, Burtin's 1956
exhibition for the USIA,
toured Kiev, Moscow,
and Tbilisi in an alternate
version, titled *Plastics
USA*, seen by 375,000
Soviet citizens in 1961.
Ezra Stoller © Esto.
All rights reserved.

The contributions made by films and newsreels issued by the USIA paled in international influence when compared to the impact of their for-profit counterparts, IDCA speakers insisted. Lucius D. Battle, the Assistant Secretary of State, announced that "cowboys and Indians have more universal appeal than anything else we have to work with in building the American image abroad because these films are the free expression of a free people, and this fact is definitely not lost on the foreigners who see them." Director George Englund agreed. "Particularly in underdeveloped countries where we generally have the worst image problem, Hollywood shoot-'em-up movies are a reflection of these people's folk heroes. What they derive from our motion pictures is a highly visible, easily understood conflict between good and evil, with good triumphing, of course." USIA chief Edward Murrow was of exactly the opposite opinion, as reported two years earlier in *Variety.* "Movies are doing a lot of harm to America," he told a gathering of Hollywood elites in 1961. "They convey the image that America is a country of millionaires and crooks."[19] Murrow's frustration was not that his agency lacked any influence upon commercial film projects, but rather that he wanted still more. As revealed by Nicholas J. Cull, the leading chronicler of USIA programs, throughout the 1950s Hollywood maintained quiet ties with the US State Department. Federal advisors regularly vetted scripts for material that might offend overseas audiences or "place America in a wrong light." A classified 1960 USIA report maintained:

> The Agency has given much attention to the task of maintaining liaison with the U.S. motion picture industry in efforts to reduce the negative impact abroad of U.S. commercial films and to improve their positive impact . . . The relationship between the Agency and the industry is delicate and highly confidential . . . However, means have been developed to exercise influence on almost all elements of the theatrical motion picture industry.[20]

In 1960, Hollywood productions drew an estimated weekly audience of 150 million foreign viewers. As a byproduct of USIA efforts to shape overseas depictions of America and its global community, the agency's motion picture interventions also were seen by as many as 32 million movie-goers in theaters across the US every week, if the agency's claim is to be believed.[21]

From the evidence presented at the 1963 IDCA, the overseas exhibition branch of the USIA was producing the agency's most positive results. "The US is doing its best image building job through cultural and trade exhibits," a design journalist reported, "attracting the best available designers and getting the most out of them."[22] At the time of the conference, about 300 USIA exhibitions circulated the world; in Eastern Europe alone over three million visitors had flocked to shows on topics as diverse as transportation, medicine, and plastics (ill.2.4). "American 'things' – packages and products – make a terrific impact on people so far as image-building is concerned," Assistant Secretary of State Battle asserted.[23] Instead of promoting ideas and concepts, far better expressed through films and publications, exhibitions showcased objects, explained IDCA speaker Jack Masey, the director of USIA East-West Exhibitions.[24] The distinction was spurious, of course. Compared to motion pictures and print media, installations of manufactured goods only *seemed* less suited to conveying broader concepts. The apparent objectivity of things made them a stellar propaganda vehicle, as amply demonstrated by Masey's achievements at the USIA.

Exhibitions produced in the early 1950s by the European Recovery Program (a.k.a. the Marshall Plan) and its successor, the Mutual Security Agency (MSA), field-tested the propaganda strategies subsequently applied around the globe by USIA exhibit designers. Divided Berlin received special attention in this regard. Until the Wall went up in 1961, East Berliners could walk to their "Free World" sister city in search of products and entertainments censured by the Party.[25] MSA information specialists exploited the city's unique political geography to pitch US campaigns directly to socialist citizens. A dream home presented at the 1952 MSA exhibition *Wir bauen ein besseres Leben* ("We're Building a Better Life") was the brainchild of Peter G. Harnden, a Yale School of Architecture graduate who, after a posting in US Army Intelligence, became a Marshall Plan and MSA exhibition designer. The "Better Life" house, a single-family home realized down to its kitchen gadgets and garden tools but missing its roof, showcased 6000 modern products, each made in a Marshall Plan partner nation. A model family portrayed by professional actors inhabited the consumer wonderland in shifts. Visitors became voyeurs, staring through windows or down from an overhead catwalk to observe the ways in which household goods shaped postwar subjects (ill.2.5). The exhibit attracted 500,000 visitors, half of them from East Germany. For the next two years it toured Stuttgart, Hanover, Paris, and Milan, spreading the message that consumption *à l'Américaine* fostered economic recovery and European cultural integration.[26]

Eisenhower championed overseas demonstrations of "ice boxes, radios, cars, how much [Americans]. . . have to eat, what they wear . . . and things like that," as he testified in Congress.[27] Ironically, the former five-star general's views clashed with those of the Republican party's Congressional majority, which championed persuasion through military hardware. As Congress trimmed the USIA budget, the Kremlin bolstered Soviet status through lavish international trade fair exhibits.[28] Recognizing a diplomacy disaster in the making, Eisenhower created a separate Office of International Trade Fairs (OITF) to remove its operations from the beleaguered USIA. By assisting US private enterprises seeking foreign markets, the OITF camouflaged propaganda activities as trade support, eluding assaults by McCarthy and associates.[29] The arrangement also reflected Eisenhower's belief that "the hand of government must be carefully concealed, and in some cases, I should say, wholly eliminated" when conducting psychological warfare.[30]

As the director of European OITF operations, Harnden produced exhibitions on a shoestring budget by artfully editing material donated by businesses into thematically coherent installations. OITF administrators in Washington would choose a theme relevant to a trade fair and its national venue; in Paris, Harnden would review the stockpile of available corporate displays, select those deemed most appropriate, and integrate them into a cohesive exhibit. Privatized cultural diplomacy turned exhibition design into a mode of bricolage bearing unintended consequences. Since exhibitions represented the US through the "found" materials of corporate donations, federal endorsement became available to any business willing to pay for the privilege. At "Main Street USA," an exhibition designed by Harnden for trade fairs in France, Spain, and Italy, a suburban dwelling furnished by a consortium of four prefabricated homebuilders and *House Beautiful* magazine represented America through pastel kitchens and plush living rooms. "Technology

2.6
The historic Kitchen Debate at the 1959 American National Exhibition in Moscow. In front, from center left to right: Soviet Premier Nikita Khrushchev, US Vice President Richard Nixon, Communist Party Central Committee Second Secretary Leonid Brezhnev, and a sunshine-yellow General Electric washer-dryer.
AP photo.

2.5
Hovering above the roofless model home at the *We're Building a Better Life* exhibit, staged in West Berlin in 1952, a narrator dressed in white coveralls explains the consumer lifestyle rituals of the installation's resident model family for postwar Germans unaccustomed to the luxurious abundance said to characterize middle-class American domesticity.

in Daily Life," produced for a trade fair in Spain, appended the "Main Street" home to industrial promotions to show the relationship of applied science to American lifestyle.[31] Harnden's recombinant installation technique achieved international fame at the USIA 1959 American National Exhibition in Moscow. Its historic "Kitchen Debate" pitted Soviet Premier Nikita Khrushchev against US Vice President Richard Nixon. Before a mob of reporters and a phalanx of sunshine-yellow appliances donated by General Electric, the world leaders argued about which of their respective economic systems would ultimately "deliver the goods" to global postwar citizens (ill.2.6).

Speakers at the 1963 IDCA questioned whether exhibitions of American plenty would ultimately alienate the citizens of poorer Asian, African, and Latin American nations. IDCA panelist Allen Hurlburt, an art director for *Look* magazine, feared that the USIA might "give the impression of a rich Uncle Sam with a button-down collar."[32] His critique

echoed historian Daniel Boorstin's account of a USIA exhibit at the 1960 Indian Agricultural Fair in New Delhi:

> One of the sights most impressive to all comers was an American farm kitchen – a dazzling porcelain-and-chrome spectacle, complete with refrigerator, disposal, deep-freeze, automatic washer and dryer, and an electric stove. Before it walked a long procession of Indian peasant women. Long pendant earrings, bangles on arms and ankles, objects piercing their noses – these pieces of gold were their savings which they dared not put in the hands of banks. In their arms they carried bare-bottomed infants. They stopped and stood in bewilderment. What was this? It was the image of America.[33]

Publisher Patwant Singh dismissed USIA initiatives that appealed to a class "already Western-oriented rather than those groups which

are indifferent . . . to the American way of life.''[34] What seemed an oversight was in fact tactical. As noted in a classified report, USIA campaigns addressed the ''more politically alert and potentially most influential citizens.''[35] Rather than relying on the public at large, as Jessica Gienow-Hecht notes of US policy in postwar Europe, US cultural propaganda often targeted local elites as ''key individuals who, it was hoped, would absorb the offerings and then pass on to a broader audience what they had learned.''[36] The same was true of Third World displays of US consumer bounty. ''Product displays are faulted as being the embodiment of a crassly materialistic society. I frankly find it difficult to understand this chagrin,'' complained Harnden in his talk on USIA exhibitions. ''Every nation in the world would like to achieve the prosperity that permits this abundance. Hair shirts aren't in order.''[37]

Environment by Design, IDCA 1970

The consumer abundance promoted globally by the USIA found a new generation of critics at the 1970 IDCA. It spun out of control with the arrival of a counterculture contingent that Reyner Banham dubbed ''the Berkeley/Ant Farm/Mad Environmentalist coalition.''[38] When its hippies demanded that the design establishment join a crusade to save the planet, the British urbanist Peter Hall refused with a mocking retort. ''You've all worn metaphorical hair shirts, even if they look impeccably styled in the West Coast idiom from where I stand . . . [S]top talking about the coming apocalypse.''[39] Hall's insistence that ecofreaks stop campaigning against environmental degradation conveys the fury of a progressive intellectual suddenly relegated to the trailing edge of social change.

For a *High Noon* duel pitting hippie environmentalists against corporate designers, no setting was more appropriate than Aspen. Once a Ute Indian summer camp at the base of the Maroon Bells mountain peaks, Aspen became a one-generation boomtown in the 1880s, as miners overran the valley to plunder its silver deposits. When prices collapsed, the population of 12,000 crashed as well. By the 1930s, residents numbered in the hundreds. ''The quiet years'' ended in the mid-1940s with the arrival of ski tourism and Walter Paepcke, CEO of the Container Corporation of America and founder, with his wife Elizabeth, of IDCA. By the 1960s, a nonconformist contingent had also discovered Aspen's allure. In 1969, resident gonzo journalist Hunter S. Thompson mobilized the town's disenfranchised hippies in a mayoral campaign for the election of Joe Edwards, a biker-cum-lawyer, on a ''Freak Power''

platform. Following Edwards' narrow defeat, Thompson ran for sheriff in 1970 (ill.2.7). He promised to change the town's name to ''Fat City'' as a means to ''prevent greedheads, land-rapers and other human jackals from capitalizing on the name 'Aspen','' make bicycles available as public transport, ''sod the streets at once,'' and direct the sheriff's office ''savagely to harass all those engaged in any form of land-rape.''[40] The incursion of Bay Area ecofreaks at the 1970 conference mirrored the ''Battle of Aspen'' being waged just outside the Institute's manicured grounds, fueling anxiety among well-heeled conference veterans who saw scrappy, long-haired activists descend upon the design establishment's Rocky Mountain stronghold.

IDCA's youth outreach program provided denim-clad barbarians with their opportunity to storm the ''Athens of the mountains.'' In 1963, a student contingent from UCLA organized four anodyne presentations on ''The American Image.'' Six years later, Northern Illinois University brought the era of youth protest to IDCA with their sculptural contribution of a stack of junked cars surrounded by cast-off toilets, tires, and home water heaters, all painted flat white. In keeping with the 1970 theme of ''Environment by Design,'' IDCA organizers invited young Northern Californian ecological activists to the conference. One was Michael Doyle, who earned a living at the landscape architecture and planning firm of Lawrence Halprin and Associates. In a memo to his boss, Doyle expressed his skepticism about IDCA. ''The conference, as it is set up, is a waste of time . . . a place where so-called great names come to pedantically disseminate their views to the less fortunate, less famous designers. Fly in – speak – fly out.'' He proposed a counter program of radical interventions:

> Have no famous speakers . . . have people in communes come and live there, Indians, have young people come and build environments for a week to live in. Have the whole conference live on the conference grounds for a week – together . . . or at one of the parks. Have foam houses, geodesics, tents, inflatables, have them build and live [in] a community . . . Aspen 1970 could be a living, breathing, viable organism that is unpredictable and let us just be its mother and nourish it to see where it goes.[41]

Doyle's strategies for disruption revealed the alienation implicit in the design profession's generational divide. The result at the 1970 IDCA was, in Banham's words, ''a guaranteed communications failure.''[42]

2.7
The election poster for Hunter S. Thompson's 1970 campaign for the office of sheriff in Aspen, designed by self-described artist/activist Tom Benton, features a badge emblazoned with a "freak power" fist clenched around a flower.

Doyle sent a copy of his memo to another member of IDCA's invited "environmental group," Cliff Humphrey, the co-founder of Berkeley's Ecology Action commune. Like many urban collectives, Ecology Action (ill.2.8) was both a residence and an enterprise. Communards ran their home as a laboratory for recycling practices that are routine today, but which were considered truly eccentric at the apogee of a throwaway consumer culture. A *New York Times Magazine* reporter catalogued their everyday routines with the fascination of an ethnographer observing an exotic tribe. Residents wore sweaters indoors rather than heat rooms to shirtsleeve temperature; they placed bricks in toilet tanks to reduce flushed water. Refusing paper bags supplied by merchants, they carried purchases home in knapsacks.[43] Rather than deposit trash in a single bin, they separated it by category for delivery to an industrial recycler. Humphrey maintained that sorting through one's own garbage not only reduced landfill waste but also reformed values. Now so commonplace that their radical dissensus is easily overlooked, the "little tactics of the habitat" devised by Ecology Action communards proclaimed that minor acts could scale up to yield major change: an approach still championed by sustainability advocates half a century later.

In the months before the 1970 IDCA, Humphrey and 50 associates walked the 600-mile length of California's Central Valley staging educational "eco-festivals" in agricultural towns. Meanwhile, an ally in the Department of Architecture at Berkeley, Sim Van der Ryn, was convening Bay Area confederates to gather for a freewheeling counterculture design festival at Freestone, a bucolic site 60 miles north of San Francisco (ill.2.9). One of those who attended, *Progressive Architecture* editor Forrest Wilson, solicited an article on the gathering. Freestoner Gordon Ashby, an emeritus of the Eames design office,

2.8
Members of the Ecology Action commune rally the citizens of Berkeley to protest air pollution in a parade of non-motorized vehicles through city streets during a commune-sponsored event, Smog-Free Locomotion Day, in September 1969.

assembled a camera-ready insert from materials contributed by the gathering's participants.[44] "Advertisements for a Counter Culture," the resulting collage of texts, freehand drawings, snapshots, and scavenged halftones printed in raw process colors, flagrantly violated the journal's slick format and reputedly cost Wilson his job.[45] The insert included a manifesto by the Ant Farm art and design collective outlining the challenges confronting hippies committed to social and ecological change. America's vaunted "standard of living" had sharpened "the difference between richest and poorest." Extractive industries and the legal fictions enacted "to protect these storehouses of fat" fostered an ecologically disastrous consumer economy. A principled response to this environmental demolition derby would launch hippies on a new journey of self-discovery. Banding in ad-hoc tribes, they might "either actively patch up their environment, or escape into less troubled lands

and ideologies." Departure from "Fat City" augured "life in teepees, earth houses, domes (the obvious technology), or the salvaged plastic of other eras."(ill.2.10) A new breed of "media nomads" would assume "many roles – actors, cowboys, clowns, pirates – in order to gain access to Fat City technology."[46] Freestone exercises in eco-ethics, eco-aesthetics, and tactics of "Fat City" disruption prepared the gathering's alumni for a Rocky Mountain showdown with the design establishment three months later.

The 1970 IDCA theme was sown with potential misunderstandings. For hippie moderns, the terms "environment" and "ecology" were synonymous, while for conference organizers "environment" simply signified the context in which designed objects existed.[47] Incongruent communication practices also separated hippie and establishment designers. Interaction at IDCA consisted of formal conference

2.9
Berkeley architecture professor Sim Van der Ryn (directly above driver, with elbow resting on the truck cab) and a posse of "outlaw builders" pose for a group portrait on their way to a construction site in rural Marin County, c.1970.

presentations and informal mixing over meals and cocktails: a formula rejected by ecofreak activists, who distributed underground publications at an outdoor bazaar, held group encounters in an Ant Farm inflatable structure, and arrived for conference sessions trailing children. Cliff Humphrey suggested a group picnic at the Aspen city dump as an object lesson in consumer waste. When the event failed to materialize, he collected garbage generated by IDCA participants for use as a visual aid during his formal presentation. The gesture was intended as both provocation and revelation. Humphrey had become an environmentalist after studying Native American anthropology at Berkeley. Transferring the study of middens from the indigenous past to contemporary Aspen, he affirmed that the empirical measure of postwar consumer society could be found in its trail of debris. Flouting the technical and cultural mechanisms devised to keep human waste unseen, Humphrey brought refuse to light – and thus to consciousness. Integrating this suppressed class of material artifacts into one's worldview constituted a radical (and radicalizing) breakthrough in perception, and a necessary component of a holistic, systems worldview. In his IDCA presentation, Humphrey proposed that the conference theme, rather than "Environment by Design," should have been "Survival by Design." Decrying the collaboration of designers "lubricated with a profit motive" in "ruining our life support system," he pleaded: "The urgency, the calamity that is confronting us has not been transmitted to you." To close the "survival gap" between throwaway mass consumption and the biosphere's carrying capacity, the design profession would need to fight for "a new economic system" in which profits were not contingent upon "destroying our environment."[48] Saul Bass, the noted graphic designer, spoke for many Aspen regulars when he implored: "Why do we have to assess capitalism? We're just trying to stage a conference!"[49]

Humphrey's plea received novel confirmation in an address by Walter Orr Roberts, a leading climatologist. Scientists, he explained, knew that the amount of carbon dioxide generated by burning fossil fuels had been "sufficient to produce substantial changes in the heat balance of the atmosphere." Indeed, atmospheric data indicated that it had already happened. "A striking change that many of us have tried to explain has been the warming trend that occurred in the northern part of our continent . . . between about 1900 and about 1950." Accumulating atmospheric carbon, while a matter of record, defied the scientific capacity to predict "whether in Aspen, or New York, or Rio de

2.10

To commemorate Earth Day in 1970, the Ant Farm underground architectural collective staged "Air Emergency," a performance art protest, on the Berkeley campus. Dressed in lab coats and gas masks, members of the collective instructed bystanders to enter a vinyl inflatable "Clean Air Pod" in order to survive a toxic "air failure:" an act of environmentalist guerrilla theater that evoked the elementary-school civil defense alerts of an atomic age childhood.

2.11
Reyner Banham cycling
along Carteret Street
in Westminster, London.
Architectural Press Archive/
RIBA Collections.

Janeiro, or Sofia, or Moscow, this is going to produce drier climate or wetter climate, warmer climate or colder climate." While much about the "fragile gaseous envelope around our earth" eluded scientists, Roberts suspected that "we may have engaged in global scale weather modification experiments without knowing it."[50] Thirty years before the term "anthropocene" first appeared in print, an unlikely assembly of industrial designers and hippie activists heard evidence of humankind's launch into an unprecedented geological epoch.[51]

At the 1970 IDCA, proponents of two avant-garde traditions, one aesthetic, the other political, rejected ecology's conceptual demands. Reyner Banham (ill.2.11), an impresario of avant-garde movements past and present, peppered his address, "The Education of an Environmentalist," with insults directed at "Sim Van der Ryn's tribes." He ranted against the most radical notion circulating among Aspen's scientists and ecofreaks:

> We will certainly have gone below the threshold of what is educationally tolerable if we produce people who think carbon dioxide is a pollutant . . . You live on carbon dioxide; it's the key link in our life cycle. Yet we talk about it as though it were some kind of dangerous pollutant. It's no more dangerous [a] pollutant than water is.[52]

Rejecting categorically the underpinnings of an anthropocene conception of the environment – that "We are as gods and might as well get good at it," as Stewart Brand proclaimed in his introduction to the *Whole Earth Catalog* – Banham complained: "We're already talking here [at Aspen] as if we and nature were equals or we were Jehovah creating the world again. We are very small environmental operators."[53]

Ecological activism proved equally repugnant to the New Left radicals of "the French group," a European IDCA contingent. Its spokesman, the Marxist sociologist and cultural critic Jean Baudrillard, thanked Banham for unmasking "the illusions of Design and Environment practice," claiming that initiatives regarding "environment, design, the fight against pollution, and so on" were "pure social manipulation" and "a new 'opium for the people.'" The "mystique of Environment" intentionally forged "a false interdependence between individuals. Nothing better than a touch of ecology and catastrophe to unite the social classes, except perhaps a witch-hunt (the mystique of anti-pollution being nothing but a variation of it)."[54]

According to Baudrillard, in protesting an economy premised upon environmental degradation, Aspen's hippie contingent was colluding in a conspiracy hatched by corporate capitalists "to mobilize people's conscience by shouting apocalypse."[55] His portrayal of ecofreaks as counter-revolutionaries, while delusional, was highly instrumental. By portraying American environmental activism as reactionary, Baudrillard asserted a French New Left monopoly on radical politics.

Baudrillard's attack came during a closing session that left Banham, its chair, "psychologically bruised," as he later confided.[56] Simmering conflicts boiled over when Michael Doyle, representing the Bay Area contingent, read out its uncompromising conference resolutions. They demanded an immediate US military withdrawal from Vietnam; a moratorium on extractive industries pending environmental impact regulation; recognition of land claims by Native Americans; an end to the persecution of Blacks, Mexican-Americans, women, and homosexuals; the legalization of abortion; a new economy based on need rather than profit; immediate federal action on the ecological crisis; and a refusal by designers to work on any product or service devised "for the sole purpose of creating profit."[57] Doyle insisted that conferees vote on the resolutions as a block; Banham countered by "picking up every point from the floor, in order to give frightened souls a chance to slip out quietly."[58] Although he ultimately succeeded in calling a clause-by-clause referendum, ensuing bitterness on all sides prompted the IDCA board to consider whether to abandon the whole conference enterprise.[59] After a vote, the board decided to continue the IDCA tradition; Eliot Noyes, confessing that the week's developments had left him "bruised, stale, and weary," resigned his position as the organization's president.[60]

With the benefit of hindsight, we now know that Baudrillard, Banham, and Hall were categorically – even cataclysmically – wrong. The ecological crisis was neither a hippie hallucination nor a delusion explained by Marxist "false consciousness." Given incontrovertible evidence that carbon dioxide is indeed a noxious pollutant; that, in the years since the 1970 IDCA, atmospheric degradation has continued racing toward catastrophe; that economic and political systems rewarding ecological destruction are to blame; and that the survival of species, economies, and ways of life is actually at stake; a re-evaluation of the provocations posed at the 1970 IDCA by its "Berkeley/ Ant Farm/Mad Environmentalist coalition" is in order. Whatever might be said about their hippie regalia, utopian philosophies, and oddball comportment, they demand reappraisal as a political and aesthetic avant-garde galvanized by their mission of inventing an everyday culture of ecological sustainability.

BUILDING MODERNIST BUT NOT QUITE CORPORATE DESIGN IN THE POSTWAR SUBURB

LOUISE A. MOZINGO

n 1954, General Foods, a *Fortune* 500 company headquartered in Manhattan for 30 years, relocated to White Plains, New York, occupying a new, custom-designed, proprietary building. The move from Manhattan to suburban Westchester County attracted enough notice to warrant a spread in *BusinessWeek* that characterized the resettlement of over 1300 employees as "Food Company Flees Madding Crowd."[1] General Foods heralded what would become over the next decades a steady march of corporate headquarters away from dense, diverse center cities towards leafy, privileged suburban peripheries.

BusinessWeek's notice of the relocation underscores the very newness of a suburban corporate headquarters. Although peripheral factory sites in industrial suburbs often included corporate offices, consolidating select top ranks of the corporate hierarchy in impressive buildings and grounds in polite, primarily residential suburbs, such as White Plains, was an unprecedented metropolitan phenomenon. These emblematic corporate-built suburban environments evolved during the 1950s and, by 1975, spread across the United States and persist to the present day. They engaged designers of national and international standing and functioned as both actual and symbolic centers for far-flung global enterprises.

From an early twenty-first-century perspective, corporate management logically followed the industry, retail, and residential development that preceded it to the suburbs. Yet the corporations that instigated relocations, the jurisdictions that accepted office development, and the architects and landscape architects who designed the projects had to invent a new suburban prototype. The optimal conception of the suburban headquarters evolved through several key projects starting in the early 1950s. In each project, the intersecting values of the corporate leaders, the designers they hired, and the politics of the communities where they located, each added particular elements to the formulation of the headquarters' site and architecture. By 1975, corporate headquarters became a recognizable American suburban development type, widely adopted by corporations, keenly coveted as commissions by designers, and enthusiastically lauded by the popular and professional press.

In becoming a customary element of the suburban landscape, the postwar suburban corporate headquarters established a distinct pattern of building and landscape steeped in a peculiarly American vision. Designing these new workplaces engaged two seemingly antithetical leitmotifs: a glinting futurism in the austere materials and space of their expansive structures and a nostalgic idyll in the lush groves and grassy slopes of their extensive landscape surrounds. Each of these, the modernist and the pastoral, served corporate interests in communicating to an array of constituents a vision of up-to-date productivity and efficiency and adherence to comfortable American values while nevertheless asserting ascendancy and power.

Suburban corporate headquarters appeared as several forces converged in business, the history of American cities, and a transformational taste in design of the built environment.[2] Essential to understanding the postwar moment for American corporations is the rise of managerial capitalism. Beginning in the 1920s, American corporations devised a management structure that set out a clear decision-making strategy in which top management commanded a hierarchy of middle managers divided into such specialties as finance, sales, production, and research and development. The middle management divisions, in turn, directed a set of lower managers distributed across the various corporate enterprises. This allowed centralized corporate staffs to manage large and diverse enterprises spread across national and global geographies, significantly increasing their productivity and profits through a rational management structure. Ideally, managerial capitalism instilled a culture of proficiency and accountability throughout the corporate enterprise. By the postwar era, managerial capitalism permeated the executive structures of most large corporations.[3]

Managerial capitalism created the conditions that supported the advent of suburban corporate headquarters and its particular design in American suburbs. Rather than relations of the company's founders and owners, it favored the promotion of professionally trained and expert managers consolidated in a clearly defined corporate echelon. By setting apart top management, managerial capitalism created a class of elite corporate executives. As competition for executives in the postwar era became fierce, workplaces that reflected their prized status became essential tools in attracting top talent to corporate enterprises.

In addition, war profits, economic dominance, and expansion made American corporations rich, bent on growth, and optimistic. The Second World War destroyed much of the industrial infrastructure of Europe and Japan, and the industries of the United States easily came to dominate the global economy, controlling 60 per cent of the world's industrial production by the late 1940s.[4] Corporations could afford to think big and build big and, to an extent, needed to do so. Corporate staffs rapidly expanded, by one estimate doubling in size between 1942 and 1952. Yet city center offices were in scarce supply after the construction hiatus of

"Designing these new workplaces engaged two seemingly antithetical leitmotifs: a glinting futurism in the austere materials and space of their expansive structures and a nostalgic idyll in the lush groves and grassy slopes of their extensive landscape surrounds."

the depression and wartime material restrictions.[5] Awash in earnings, corporations could consider and afford building new facilities.

The questions then became where to build and how to build. Downtown locations remained advantageous and appealing for many corporations. The proximity of bankers, brokerage houses, capital investors, and associated services such as advertising, law, and accounting firms in central business districts induced some expanding corporations to choose, or maintain, downtown locations. There they often leased old or new office space but also sometimes occupied elegant custom-built modernist skyscrapers, such as the justifiably lauded 1952 Lever House in Manhattan designed by Skidmore, Owings & Merrill.[6] Nevertheless, for a significant number of postwar enterprises, the seeming advantages of the bucolic edge outweighed the more proven draws of the central business district.[7]

Unlike their pre-war predecessors, corporations had reasons to consider a much larger geographic area for their new offices. New state and federal highway projects extended out and around major American cities and, in the process, absorbed large tracts of formerly rural land into the economic geography of metropolitan regions.[8] This allowed corporations to buy larger parcels of land to build their own facilities, not only to accommodate their current staff but to expand those offices as needed, difficult if not impossible to do in the built-out central business districts. Sites distant from center cities mitigated a perceived threat particular to the postwar era, atomic destruction. Even before the war's end, the federal government had been calling for industrial dispersion to decrease urban congestion and vulnerability to bombardment, an impulse that accelerated after the targeting of Nagasaki and Hiroshima in August 1945.[9] As *Fortune* reported in 1952, 22 companies in Manhattan contemplating suburban moves did so in part because of concerns about remaining in "target areas."[10] As residential subdivisions spread across the suburban periphery, the concentration of desirable corporate labor shifted as well. In this, corporations were seeking not only potential up-and-coming male executives but, more critically, the well-educated women who composed the vast clerical staffs that served the corporate hierarchy.[11] In both cases, corporations sought personnel that in 1952 *Fortune* cagily referred to as "a better type" – white and unequivocally middle or upper middle class.[12]

In seeking space, distance, and labor in the periphery, businesses followed influential corporate precedents. By 1950 two prominent technology corporations, AT&T Bell Laboratories and General Electric,

3.1
The General Foods Headquarters after the completion of the Cross-Westchester Parkway and an expansion of the original buildings.

had completed large purpose-built, corporate-owned suburban facilities for their research and development staffs. Another, for General Motors, was well underway. Research and development personnel occupied an elevated regard even within middle management because of their much sought-after expertise. Corporations zealously competed with government laboratories and universities, both of which rapidly expanded in the postwar years, for bright research scientists and engineers. In response, corporations devised suburban "corporate campuses" explicitly modeled on typical American university settings where ample landscape surrounds enclosed stately buildings.

Corporations were convinced that the landscape settings of their campuses attracted the best engineers and scientists and fostered innovation.[13] For a century, Frederick Law Olmsted and his followers unflaggingly promoted pastoral public parks, college campuses, and suburban residential enclaves as the scenic antidote to the industrial city's real and perceived ills. Pastoral taste permeated the values of corporate leaders. As *BusinessWeek* remarked of the AT&T and GE campuses: "Work goes on in a campus-like atmosphere that the brainy youngsters seem to go for."[14] By the 1950s this received wisdom pervaded corporate thinking, even to the point of stretching the limits of credulity. One executive contemplating a suburban move for corporate offices confidently told *Fortune*: "Everybody can work better and think better in the country."[15]

General Foods's migration to White Plains began in 1948 as it realized that a staff of 1200 spread across three Manhattan buildings needed a consolidated office space to maximize its organizational capacity. Space in Manhattan was scarce and at a premium. Expecting to accommodate a significantly larger number of employees in the near future, the corporation started exploring peripheral sites in the New York area. Discarding areas in both New York and New Jersey with suburban industries, the corporate leaders scouted the location of AT&T Bell Labs' corporate campus, the well-established, upper middle-class suburb of Summit, New Jersey. General Foods settled on the White Plains site in Westchester County and hired Bell Labs' architectural designers, the firm of Voorhees, Walker, Foley, and Smith. The company decided that the advantages of building a new facility outweighed the many added costs that it would incur in land acquisition, construction, staff transitions, and ongoing maintenance.[16]

Westchester County exemplifies a quintessentially American pastoral landscape taste inextricably linked to white, upper-class values.[17] Long the territory of the horsey estates of the New York elite, the choice deliberately allied General Foods with the county's long-standing reputation as an exclusive enclave. The site itself lay adjacent to hospital grounds designed by Olmsted, and was strategically visible along what was to become the Cross-Westchester Parkway. During the nineteenth century Olmsted and his allies had promoted parkways as recreational roadways lined with trees, grassy verges, and medians to connect urban park sites across growing industrial cities. Examples appeared in Buffalo, Boston, Chicago, and Kansas City.[18] In the twentieth century, Westchester County had been an experiment ground for parkway systems intended to extend from the city into the countryside as a means for recreational automobile trips along limited-access, carefully graded and planted, wide, curving rights of way, devoid of billboards and commercial establishments.[19] Planned but not yet quite completed when General Foods took up residence in 1954, the arcing parkway at the site's edge would perfectly display the new headquarters to the passing motorists on what would become a major automobile commuter route.

General Foods's management chose the site because it was flexibly large, agreeably prestigious, and visibly prominent.[20] The status-conscious local residents, however, raised vociferous objections to

"Everybody can work better and think better in the country."

the new development. Large employment centers did not fit into the genteel suburban image of White Plains and the leisure-class county. Yet the expansion of residential subdivisions that were breaking apart the county's large estates and rural land proved to be an ever-rising burden on local services as residential taxes did not meet the rapidly rising fiscal costs of a growing population. Fearful of higher taxes, or, worse, noxious and blue-collar manufacturing, county politicians allied themselves with General Foods, eager for their revenues and reassuringly white-collar employees.[21] The mayor of White Plains, Edward Michaelian, who later served for decades as the Westchester County Executive, carefully negotiated between the corporation and his constituents. After a hearing described by Michaelian as the most contentious of his 30-year career, the project moved forward attached to stringent new zoning ordinances. Building height limits of three stories, on-site parking, and most importantly, generous landscape setbacks, which the public perceived as congruent with the county's prevailing scenery, quelled the opposition.[22]

The resulting headquarters adhered to the local jurisdictional requirements and set in place site planning parameters that would be reiterated in future suburban corporate headquarters. Voorhees, Walker, Foley, and Smith designed a brick-clad building with a restrained modernist inflection reminiscent of Eliel Saarinen's famous structures at Cranbrook Academy and similar to Bell Labs in Summit, New Jersey.[23] The brick exterior, even if deployed in a contemporary manner, adhered to a common east-coast vernacular extending back to the colonial era. Initially the building surrounded three sides of a courtyard whose open side faced the planned parkway. By the late 1950s, the staff grew so large that the firm designed a substantial addition to the original complex, a clean arc of white stone enclosing the fourth side of the courtyard, creating an imposing view from the completed parkway. An entrance driveway verged by trees and lawn swept to an eye-catching entrance of an imposing yet low-rise building complex. At both sides, two large parking areas well planted with trees flanked the building complex away from the entrance view. An ample, sloping landscape space surrounded the whole site (ill.3.1).

General Foods's site plan components – a large site, a single building complex arrived at with a sweeping driveway, two large parking areas tucked away from the entrance facade, and an enclosing landscape surround – proved to be a basic model for suburban corporate headquarters that remains to the present day. In its initial justifications for pursuing new suburban facilities, General Foods emphasized the spaciousness, efficiency, and autonomy of the new headquarters. The corporation would have the capacity to determine its own future, free from the restrained conditions of downtown.[24] As they approached the move, they underscored to a much greater degree the aesthetics of the setting, describing the move to its employees as "Out of the city . . . and into the trees."[25] The groves of trees and sloping lawn reinterpreted in a new context and for a new purpose the pastoral ideal promoted by Olmsted the century before, visible in the hospital site next door and the remaining country estates and growing suburbs of Westchester County. Most handily, the landscape both appeased the wary natives and rewarded the dedicated employees.

By the time General Foods occupied their White Plains headquarters, Connecticut General Life Insurance Company was also building a massive new office on 280 acres near Bloomfield outside of Hartford, Connecticut.[26] Highly successful under the leadership of Frazar B. Wilde, Connecticut General had expanded rapidly, increasing staff levels to unprecedented numbers. Like General Foods, Wilde wanted a corporate-owned site, to accommodate staff expansion and manage the company's future, free of constraints. Even more than other corporate staffs, Connecticut General relied on legions of women clerical workers to handle reams of documents – records of proposals, policies, claims, and payouts. Wilde had a specific idea that paper processing should be carried out in a streamlined horizontal layout, passing paper from one desk to the next, much in the same way assembly lines worked in manufacturing.[27]

While Wilde was inspired by the spare efficiency of the horizontal factory, he had two other particular considerations for a new headquarters. First, he and the Connecticut General management were extremely conscious that the setting should appeal to the many women who carried on the core of Connecticut General's business – the new headquarters had to be convincingly white-collar and not appear to be a factory.[28] Second, he was "an ardent naturalist" and wanted the grounds to reflect his interest in conservation and scenic preservation.[29]

Wilde hired the firm of Skidmore, Owings & Merrill and worked with the firm's architect Gordon Bunshaft who had designed Lever House, the landmark mid-century modernist Manhattan skyscraper that debuted with much acclaim in both the popular and professional press. Committed to the International architectural aesthetic, Bunshaft and the Skidmore, Owings & Merrill team designed a strikingly unadulterated building of steel and glass for Connecticut General. Light permeated the interiors through floor-to-ceiling windows encasing the external walls and four interior courtyards. No desk was more than 60 feet from natural light. Thanks to new structural devices and the three-story structure, the floorplates remained open span, allowing for maximum flexibility for workspace arrangements, an efficiency borrowed from the factory.[30]

While the building explicitly reinterpreted the straightforward engineering aesthetic of the factory as elegantly lustrous, fitting for efficient headquarters' employees, the enclosing landscape recalled a long-standing, and much more sentimental, elite aesthetic (ill.3.2). Completed by Skidmore, Owings & Merrill's in-house landscape architect Joanna Diman, the site design explicitly reinterpreted not only the tranquil, tended pastoral aesthetic promoted by Olmsted and his followers in the nineteenth-century public parks movement but also the eighteenth-century aesthetic of the English landscape garden estates that inspired them. Rolling lawn, clusters of trees, and a constructed lake with an eye-catching island recalling the celebrated scenery of the English estate of Blenheim, the landscape enveloped the corporate offices with unprecedented luxury. Sculpture by Isamu Noguchi added

the finishing flourish of a contemporary landscape folly. The landscape architecture formed a splendid foreground for views into the site as well as stunning vistas from the floor-to-ceiling glass within the building (ill.3.3). Fundamentally, the site plan was similar to General Foods, a dramatic driveway arriving at a distinguished building, two extents of parking at its flanks, and a pastoral surround, yet executed with a no-holds-barred generosity of space and detail.

Whereas General Foods initially employed the surrounding landscape as an instrument in negotiating local politics and, later, as an enticement for dislocated employees, the landscape at Connecticut General proved to be a boon for the company's public relations. The extraordinary combination of the lush, time-honored landscape design and gleaming, contemporary structure captured considerable attention among business leaders, the local community, politicians, and the general public. The popular, design, and business press widely covered the new headquarters.[31] Unlike General Foods, Connecticut General garnered expansive praise from design critics as a triumphant exemplar of modernist design. At the same time, however trendsetting the architecture, the landscape was even more lauded as "the English kind of countryside that Constable painted and Thomas Hardy wrote about: ancient, thrilling oaks, meadows, rows of ridge lines rising like wave crests from shallow misty valleys."[32] With Connecticut General, the American capitalist corporation mustered its place in the long history of the patrician estate.

The accolades inspired Wilde to convene a city planning conference at the new headquarters attended by Connecticut Governor Abraham Ribicoff, the famed city planner Louis Mumford, the developer Victor Gruen, and Wilfrid Owen of the Brookings Institution, among 400 others. The conference reiterated city planning precepts common in the postwar era: the wisdom of regional planning for industrial, commercial, and residential decentralization in suburbanized peripheries supported by new roadway construction and the concomitant optimized redevelopment of center cities. More remarkably, by convening the conference at their new facility, the corporation promoted their new headquarters as a model of the future of American cities writ large and cast the corporate headquarters as a project in the public interest.[33] *LIFE* (then at the peak of its circulation) devoted six pages to the conference graced by ten spectacular photographs by Ezra Stoller, nine of which were of the building's exterior.[34]

3.2
The Connecticut General
Life Insurance Company
headquarters, in Bloomfield,
Connecticut outside of
Hartford, opened in 1956.
Ezra Stoller © Esto.

3.3 overleaf
View of the pastoral
landscape as seen from the
window of the Connecticut
General Life Insurance
Company headquarters
in suburban Hartford.
Ezra Stoller © Esto.

Connecticut General institutionalized the suburban headquarters as an equally impressive alternative to the downtown skyscraper. In the immediate period after occupying the building, Wilde asserted that the new headquarters had turned out to be a very good business investment, citing increased productivity and employee retention.[35] Skidmore, Owings & Merrill went on to design numerous projects modeled after Connecticut General, for clients including the Kimberley-Clark Corporation, Neenah-Menasha, Wisconsin, 1957; the Reynolds Metal Company, Richmond, Virginia, 1957, with Charles Gillette; General Mills, Golden Valley, Minnesota, 1959; and the Upjohn Corporation (ill.3.4), Kalamazoo, Michigan, with Sasaki, Walker and Associates, 1961.

If the success of Connecticut General had one caveat it was that the site design had woefully underestimated the impact of employees'

reliance on the automobile to travel to and from work. The parking areas that flanked the building extended in size as employees eschewed the shuttles that the company initially provided from Hartford and rows of autos dominated the interior views from two sides of the building. By the time Connecticut General added onto the building a decade later, they also had to build a parking structure so as to not completely overrun the site with parking lots.[36]

Nevertheless Connecticut General demonstrated the potentials of a new design idiom that displayed a winning image of the corporation to an unexpected array of corporate constituents. The celebrated photographer W. Eugene Smith, sent by Henry Luce on assignment to photograph Connecticut General, captured the moment in an image published in *Architectural Forum* of young families looking across the lake towards the gleaming building, at ease in the land of the corporation

3.5

The renowned photographer
W. Eugene Smith captures
the grand aspiration of
postwar American society,
and capitalism, in the
family gazing at Connecticut
General's lustrous steel
corporate structure framed
by a verdant, tranquil
pastoral landscape.
Connecticut General
Life Building as printed
in *Architectural Forum*,
September 1957.
Photograph by W. Eugene
Smith.

(ill.3.5). As other corporations followed suit, they refined the fusion of an embracing landscape and an austere building and fully exploited the imageability of the suburban headquarters as a centerpiece of corporate identity.

The Deere & Company Administrative Center in Moline, Illinois, opened in 1964.[37] From its initial conception in 1956, Deere's chief executive officer, William Hewitt, intended the new headquarters to perform as a strategic instrument in achieving market dominance in the company's business, farm machinery. The company's top brass had worked for generations in modest accommodations within one of Deere's original factory sites in downtown Moline. Hewitt, who took over the company in 1955, identified the construction of a new headquarters as essential to the competitive future of the business. Impressed with GM's corporate campus outside of Detroit, Hewitt hired its architect,

Eero Saarinen, to design the headquarters and Sasaki, Dawson, DeMay of Boston to complete the landscape design on 850 acres Deere bought outside of Moline.[38]

What resulted was a spectacular reworking of the site in which the office building straddled a shallow wooded valley forming one edge of a constructed lake, a watery mirror to the structure's surprising facade (ill.3.6). Saarinen designed the building to be clad in structural members of the then new Cor-ten steel which rusts to a protective finish – a bold decision, as Hewitt's board, top executives, and employees considered the building's rusty exterior with alarmed skepticism.[39] The oxidized Cor-ten girders held a five-story box of gold-infused glass extending up from the surface of the water. Originally, a single display pavilion extended from one side of the main office building, eventually complemented by an office addition on the other side, each connected

3.6
The Administrative Center
buildings sited across
the ravine of the Deere
& Company property.
Friedman Collection Slide,
Environmental Design
Visual Resources Center,
University of California,
Berkeley.

to the main building by a spanning bridge. No architectural design had
ever pushed the boundaries of the engineering aesthetic, the "honest"
materiality of modernist design, to such an extent.

If the building challenged the limits of acceptable modernist
architectural design, the landscape soothed. Hewitt intended the site
to not only be an appropriate setting for corporate employees, but
also a welcome place for visits by the company's Midwestern farmer
customers, the foundational bedrock of Deere's business. To insure
the poised integration of landscape and architecture, early in the
design process the landscape architects went to the extent of raising
balloons at the proposed locations of the structures' corners.[40] As a
result, the luxuriant surrounding acreage seamlessly enclosed the
building in a tended, genteel pastoral landscape explicitly inspired by
the fine unsparing design of Olmsted's public parks in Boston. Unlike
Connecticut General's setting, topography and trees thoroughly hid the
large parking lots from any prospect within the building or along the
exquisitely placed, long curving driveway that unfurled the grand site
and building to approaching visitors and employees (ill.3.7).

Hewitt opened the Administrative Center in 1964, by which time
he had led the company to multinational dominance. After an inaugural
party covered by the national press and attended by a host of business
luminaries, including David Rockefeller, the president of Chase
Manhattan Bank, the Administrative Center became the manifest center
of the global corporation, featured liberally in the company's marketing
materials.[41] The meticulously constructed and maintained nature-on-
view impressed, yet proved entirely and comfortably familiar (ill.3.8).[42]
In a famous follow-up study conducted by the sociologists Mildred
and Edward Hall, Deere's employees expressed appreciation for the
building's new efficiencies and appointments but, by far, they most
valued the site's sumptuous landscape surround. Recruitment
announcements that featured the site yielded higher response rates,
and Deere's ads to encourage visitors proudly bannered "It's not just
another day at the office" above images of the structure enveloped
in greenery and reflected by the lake (ill.3.9).[43] As the Administrative
Center's daring structure and bountiful grounds garnered multiple
design awards and worldwide recognition, the corporation
headquartered in an obscure, small, Midwestern town found itself the
center of international acclaim.[44]

3.7
View of the drive into the Deere & Company Administrative Center. It shows how the design of the grading, planting and roadway maximized the aesthetic effect of the landscape surrounding the headquarters.

3.8
The entry view of the Deere & Company Administrative Center. Used in countless publications including annual reports, corporate brochures, and now websites, the Administrative Center became the icon of the global corporation for both internal and external audiences.

3.9
The executive dining room
of the Deere & Company
Administrative Center,
on the lowest floor of the
main building, level with the
water in the ponds.

By the late 1960s, after the much publicized, pioneering corporate ventures of the previous decade and a half, moves to suburban headquarters accelerated as the center of American cities became the setting of riots, revolts, political protests and obvious racial tensions, which business establishments viewed with great alarm. Coupled with the social unrest were the dispiriting effects of block clearance for redevelopment schemes and new highway construction, plus a wave of deindustrialization in older urban cores, all of which left many center cities in tatters. With these new impetuses for corporations to exit the city, the news media dubbed the hastened business departures as the "corporate exodus."[45]

After General Foods's groundbreaking establishment in 1954, a set of corporations followed and a stretch of the Cross-Westchester Parkway between White Plains and Rye Brook became known as the Platinum Mile.[46] In the move that exemplified the late 1960s corporate flight, PepsiCo traded their stylish, award-winning 1960 Manhattan headquarters designed by Skidmore, Owings & Merrill (see pl.29), to occupy a new site on 112 acres in Purchase, New York, in 1972. The unremarkable modernist building complex of broad bands of white cladding and dark glass designed by Edward Durell Stone, Sr. sat in the center of a much more outstanding landscape planned by Edward Durell Stone, Jr. and designed in detail by Russell Page, a landscape architect well known for his elegant, upscale garden designs. The site plan reiterated the elements seen in previous versions of suburban headquarters – a ceremonial entrance drive, low-rise building, and long blocks of parking carefully nestled within woodlands, well shrouded from views from the building and sculpture garden (ill.3.11).

As another wide-ranging global company, PepsiCo extended the idea of symbolic center to include corporate patronage, welcoming the public to grounds filled with a substantial collection of twentieth-century sculpture. Page devised a precisely curving path of golden gravel through the meticulously crafted bucolic setting for the many sculptures, complete with sloping lawns, tranquil glades, and shady copses (ill.3.12).[47]

While PepsiCo embraced the visiting public, albeit within the exclusive confines of upper middle-class Westchester County, a host of other corporations used their suburban moves to retreat from the public view and settle within acres of buffering woodlands. The design for the 1971 American Can headquarters in Greenwich, Connecticut, by Skidmore, Owings & Merrill and Sasaki, Dawson, DeMay eliminated visible automobiles altogether and placed the parking underground, ensuring a completely encompassing landscape setting on the 175-acre former estate (ill.3.10).[48] The project was much praised by the *New York Times* architectural critic Ada Louise Huxtable as a "a setting of idyllic splendor . . . It offers comfort, efficiency, and structural grand luxe, tastefully controlled."[49] In 1975, Richardson-Merrell soon followed American Can to Wilton, Connecticut. Designed by Kevin Roche John Dinkeloo Associates, the plan confined parking to the roof.[50] In an era of considerable questioning of corporate motivations and ethics, and deteriorating urban conditions epitomized by a center city abandoned by affluent residents and businesses, corporations regarded escape into an embracing suburban arcadia to be a tactical retreat. With every office looking out onto acres of New England woods worthy of Thoreauvian praise, urban strife could seem very far away indeed.

3.10
The American Can corporate
estate from 1971.
Ezra Stoller © Esto.

3.11
View of the PepsiCo World Headquarters in Purchase, NY, from the interior of the site.

3.12
The "golden path" connects the artworks of the Donald M. Kendall Sculpture Garden.

3.13 overleaf
Richardson Merrell Headquarters, another corporate estate tucked deep into New England woods.

By 1971, the Weyerhaeuser Corporation relocated to a new suburban headquarters outside of Tacoma, Washington, the first designed with the grandeur of its Midwest and east coast counterparts. The site and building design formed part of a public relations effort to reposition the century-old timber products company in an era of increasing environmental concerns.[51] Charles Basset of Skidmore, Owings & Merrill's San Francisco office worked with Peter Walker of the SWA Group to design a spectacular 1600-acre site in which a layered concrete building spanned a wide shallow valley. On one side of the structure, the landscape design extended a lake along the valley floor surrounded by a wetland planting, on the other a wildflower meadow. Both sides opened long views across the site. Sills of parking tiered up the two sides of the valley with densely planted slopes in between. Planters thickly bedded with cascading vines lined the edges of each floor of the structure. Reforested indigenous woodlands encompassed the remainder of the property (ill.3.14). Flourishing greenery saturated the entire complex, suffusing even the building.[52] Edged by long stretches of both a state highway and an interstate, the verdant site appeared to multitudes of passing motorists as an embodiment of the Weyerhaeuser's newly adopted tagline "The Tree Growing Company."

By the 1980s scores of corporations had moved to palatial suburban headquarters, all in one way or another a testament to the influential model developed after 1950. While nuances based on the specific taste and needs of corporate leadership, the dictates of the site, prevalent public relations concerns, and pacification of local opposition inflected design specifics, their fundamental schemes remained the same. For designers, they represented very substantial commissions, especially so for landscape architects. These corporate palaces and gardens emerged at a particular moment in which profits, political dominance, and an unflagging taste for spare structures and tranquil landscapes that signaled orderly efficiency and well-being cohered to form icons of the American capitalist enterprise. These buildings and landscapes became keystones in new public relations efforts to persuade boards, stockholders, competitors, local communities, and the general public of the worth and rightness of the corporate endeavor.

As global economic disruptions significantly reordered American enterprises by the late 1980s, corporations found themselves on shifting grounds. Tellingly, many headquarters were abandoned and some, like Connecticut General and American Can, awkwardly repurposed after threats of demolition of the structures raised an outcry from historic preservationists.[53] Others, like Upjohn, were torn down altogether. A few, like Deere & Company, maintain their splendor. Most surprisingly, Weyerhaeuser announced in 2015 that it planned to vacate its building outside Tacoma and move to downtown Seattle as, in the current received wisdom, center cities are now where the next generation of "brainy youngsters" are congregating.

Nevertheless, the current nexus of profligate global profits, Silicon Valley, has become the location of yet another manifestation of palatial corporate edifices and extensive landscape surrounds as Apple, Facebook, and Google have undertaken massively costly building projects on large sites after decades of comparative thriftiness. (Apple's new headquarters is estimated to cost a minimum of $5 billion.[54]) The impetus for powerful entities to build big is an ancient one. Whether royalty, aristocracy, religion, government, or the corporation, the built environment ultimately becomes the locus of their own self-regard to command not just a massive structure, but a massive view. In suburban corporate headquarters the amalgamation of trendsetting architecture inspired by industrial engineering and soothingly anachronistic landscape inspired by a nineteenth-century idealization of nature sums up a kind of surety in the American corporate project that encompasses both efficient business innovation and scenic territorial amplitude. It conflates, if not reconciles, two ideals of the American experiment that Alexis de Tocqueville had noted the century before and despaired of in the long term – capitalist commerce and bountiful landscapes.

3.14
View of the Weyerhaeuser
Corporate Headquarters
that opened in 1971
outside of Tacoma,
Washington.
Photo courtesy of PWP
Landscape Architecture.

DESIGN EDUCATION AT STANFORD
THE FORMATIVE YEARS

STEVEN McCARTHY

One cannot reflect on today's design education at Stanford – with its globally admired "d.school," its successful alumni, its world-class faculty, its impact on design thinking as a creative method and as a business-competitive advantage – without consideration of the many contributors, the giants on whose shoulders others perch. This includes the faculty, students, staff, resources, facilities, courses, technologies, projects and designs, and the social, cultural, and economic forces that provided a contextual frame.

A historical treatment of this subject has to start around the middle of the twentieth century, 1949 to be precise. It was then that Matthew Seymour Kahn began his lengthy career as an instructor in the Department of Art and Architecture. Hired fresh from the Cranbrook Academy of Art, Professor Kahn became quite a force at Stanford. He eventually influenced and inspired art and mechanical engineering students for six full decades. To assert that design at Stanford began with Matt Kahn is hardly an exaggeration.

Over the next two decades, a new model for design education developed on campus: the expression, subjectivity, and communicative and aesthetic qualities of art were coupled with engineering's concerns with functionality, objectivity, materials, and technology. Art and Architecture (which was later called the Department of Art, and is now Art and Art History) and the Department of Mechanical Engineering collaborated on a joint graduate program in design that emphasized visual thinking, creative problem-solving, need-finding, user-centeredness and entrepreneurial ventures. Design education at Stanford grew from this core humanistic relationship.

To return to Kahn's seminal role, he spent the 1950s involved in a prolific design practice in addition to his teaching responsibilities. His curriculum vitae stated: "Maintains a studio practice in painting. Maintains a free-lance design practice in decorative and useful articles, display interiors, graphic design, jewelry and textiles."[1] Kahn's productivity was both high quantity and high quality. He designed and screen-printed textiles for Konwiser, Inc., a "design-aware commercial company,"[2] that were acquired into the permanent collection of the Cooper Hewitt, Smithsonian Design Museum and exhibited at the Museum of Modern Art in New York.

Kahn was perhaps best known professionally for interior designs for housing manufacturer Eichler Homes. He created "sculptural and decorative designs" for Eichler in 1955 and in 1956 was the "art coordinator" of Eichler's experimental X-100 steel house that was built in San Mateo. Kahn consulted with Eichler Homes until 1962, providing such services as "color coordination" and "miscellaneous design research."[3]

Kahn also owned an Eichler house at 834 Santa Fe Avenue, just above Stanford's campus, that featured his own stunning interiors, artworks and exotic artifacts (ill.4.1), and embodied the designed life he shared with his wife Lyda, a frequent collaborator. Generations of Stanford design students recall the home fondly, as it was there that Kahn hosted his annual Halloween carved-pumpkin celebration and his weekly graduate seminar Advanced Creative Studies – the latter typically consisting of Kahn dispensing aged sherry with his sage advice.

4.1
Matt Kahn with students and faculty in his Eichler home.

"Art and Architecture and the Department of Mechanical Engineering collaborated on a joint graduate program in design that emphasized visual thinking, creative problem-solving, need-finding, user-centeredness and entrepreneurial ventures. Design education at Stanford grew from this core humanistic relationship."

4.2
John Arnold in his Stanford
office.

In 1957, another sagacious pillar of design education was installed at Stanford: John Edward Arnold (ill.4.2) was hired away from the Massachusetts Institute of Technology (MIT) to teach in the Department of Mechanical Engineering. With a proven record of innovative teaching and research that drew from psychology, science fiction, creativity studies, and business, Professor Arnold is credited with establishing the Department of Mechanical Engineering's Design Division.

The statement "Arnold sought to balance the then prevalent analytical approach to technology with an approach based on synthesis. . ."[4] suggests that Arnold's thrust formed a symbiosis with Kahn's multifaceted creative practice, revealing the double roots of design at Stanford. Besides providing experience and leadership to a growing engineering design program, Arnold's best legacy may have been the hiring of mechanical engineering professor Robert "Bob" McKim in 1958 (ill.4.3).

John Arnold died unexpectedly in 1963 en route to Rome while on sabbatical leave. He had planned to use the time away to write a book on "the philosophy of engineering."[5] The memorial resolution read to the Stanford University Faculty Senate stated that Arnold "believed in generalism – his concept of the 'ultimate designer' stressed fluency of thought and zest for technology on a broad spectrum."[6] McKim inherited this notion and furthered it.

McKim held an engineering degree from Stanford and an industrial design degree from Pratt Institute in New York, both at the bachelor's level. He and Matt Kahn would cement the joint graduate program in design between mechanical engineering and art over the next few years, conferring MS and MA degrees respectively. To prepare for this larger vision, Kahn embarked on an ambitious trip during the summer of 1959.

4.3
Robert McKim with students.

4.5
Student-designed "Motor Hoop," 1967.

4.4 previous pages
Design Division students on their water crafts, 1967.

4.6
Robert McKim standing next to the Imaginarium.

Keen to learn more about design education at institutions with more established programs, Kahn visited nine schools in lieu of attending the annual International Design Conference at Aspen that year. He traveled to Harvard, Yale, Columbia, Cooper Union, Pratt, MIT, Carnegie Institute of Technology (now Carnegie Mellon University), the Illinois Institute of Technology (IIT) and the School of the Art Institute of Chicago. His final report stated:

I return to Stanford with the feeling that we should have a rich offering in design in which the traditional crafts play a disciplined part. Regionally, an interest in the products of "design" has reached an intensity which is of cultural significance, with many designers and craftsmen practicing in this area. I believe that a program at Stanford which would reflect and tap this could be an important part of our identity, and that it would attract good students who are finding it difficult to get this kind of training.[7]

The 1960s saw the hiring of new mechanical engineering faculty as the Design Division grew. Added in particular were assistant professors Bernard "Bernie" Roth in 1962, who turned down a faculty position at his alma mater Columbia University, and James L. "Jim" Adams in 1966, who brought his five years' experience at the Jet Propulsion Laboratory and year studying art at UCLA to the mix. McKim's humanistic imprint on the program grew, as evidenced in the course description from ME 112b, Introduction to Product Design, from 1966: "Active encounter with human values in design. Lectures survey central philosophy of product design program, with emphasis upon the relation between technical and human values, the creative process, and design methodology."[8]

Besides notable faculty, design at Stanford was also enabled by unorthodox philosophies and environments. The sixties witnessed faculty forays into the Esalen Institute's human potential movement, to "rediscover the miracle of self-aware consciousness" at their Big Sur retreat center on the Pacific coast.[9] McKim's experiments with the hallucinogen LSD were noted in *What the Dormouse Said: How the Sixties Counterculture Shaped the Personal Computer Industry*.[10] The Imaginarium, a 16-foot geodesic dome, was used for class audio-visual stimulation exercises with the hope of expanding students' creative abilities (ill.4.6). The Loft, the funky and 'lived-in' graduate student studio space, gave decades of students' creative endeavors a physical home – it is still thriving today.

In the 1970s, McKim and Adams published important books that built on Arnold's earlier ideas about creativity: *Experiences in Visual Thinking* (1972) and *Conceptual Blockbusting: A Guide to Better Ideas* (1974), respectively. In 1976 Larry Leifer returned to Stanford – having earned his MS here in 1964 as one of "three graduates in the first cohort"[11] – as an associate professor with co-appointments in medicine and engineering. Art bolstered its design faculty in the 1970s by hiring Jan Molenkamp, a Yale-educated graphic designer who went on to design for Hewlett-Packard.

The 1970s produced some of the design 'rock stars' that Stanford is famous for. David Kelley, co-founder of the global design consultancy IDEO and current Stanford professor, graduated in 1978. In a handwritten note to Matt Kahn, he wrote, "You have been such an inspiration to me. You see things the rest of us never will – and say things I only wish I could. You have changed me. Thank you."[12] Harley Jessup completed his MFA in 1978 with a thesis titled "Graphic Sequences,"[13] and went on to win an Academy Award for best visual effects for the film *Innerspace*. Bill Hill headed the San Francisco office of MetaDesign, winning accolades for his interaction designs for corporations including Wells Fargo, Adobe and Sony. Dean Hovey was Kelley's first business partner – the pair created early designs for Apple.

There are some ties between Stanford design and the subject of international corporate design: Bob McKim worked for the office of Henry Dreyfuss; Jim Adams "was fortunately known by Henry Dreyfuss" through personal connections.[14] Both McKim and Adams worked briefly at General Motors. In 1964 Matt Kahn proposed a workshop for General Motors, in which he would "administer a sort of therapeutic bombardment to your automotive designers,"[15] and in 1972 finally visited GM in Warren, Michigan, giving his signature slide lecture "Design – Body and Soul."

This never-before-examined historical slice of design education at Stanford describes its foundations and trajectory from mid-century through the 1970s. While professional designers and their corporate clients of this same era were embracing the International Style vocabulary that was dominant at the time, Stanford faculty were focusing on nourishing students' bodies and souls with a bold vision, an innovative curriculum, new creative methodologies, and inspiring research and professional practice.

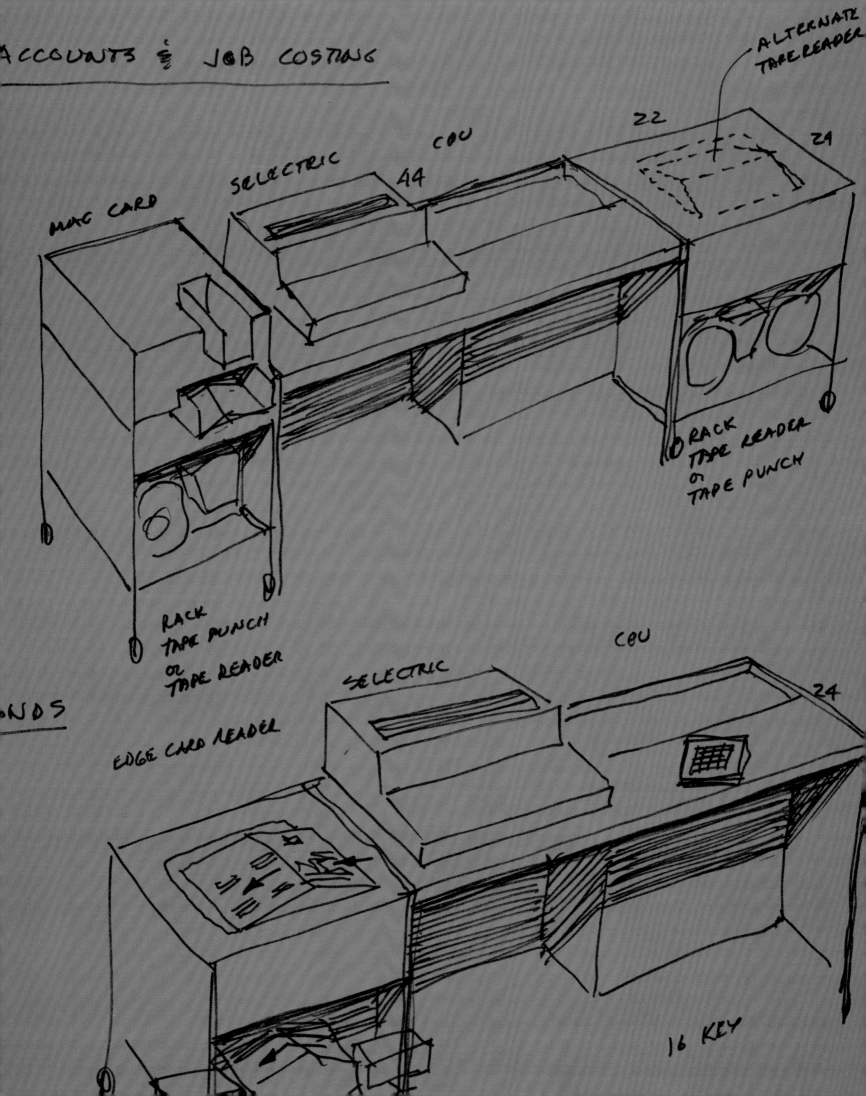

ACCOUNTS & JOB COSTING

ALTERNATE TAPE READER

22   24

CPU

SELECTRIC   44

MAG CARD

RACK
TAPE READER
or
TAPE PUNCH

RACK
TAPE PUNCH
or
TAPE READER

NDS

EDGE CARD READER

SELECTRIC   CPU

24

16 KEY

MAJOR OBJECTS IN THE EXHIBITION *CREATIVITY ON THE LINE*

1.
Gyula Pap, Floor lamp, *c.*1923.
Nickel-plated metal, glass and
black-lacquered iron.
Height: 177.48 cm (69 ⅞ in),
diameter 35.56 cm (14 in).
Los Angeles County Museum of
Art, Los Angeles, California. Gift
of Debbie and Mark Attanasio,
in memory of Barbara Kaplan
(M.2007.98).

2.
Carl-Ernst Hinkefuss, Cover of
Qualität, vol.9 (1931), nos 3–4,
devoted to the German
company AEG (Allgemeine
Elektrizitätsgesellschaft).
Print on coated paper.
29.5 x 20.9 cm (11 ⅝ x 8 ¼ in).

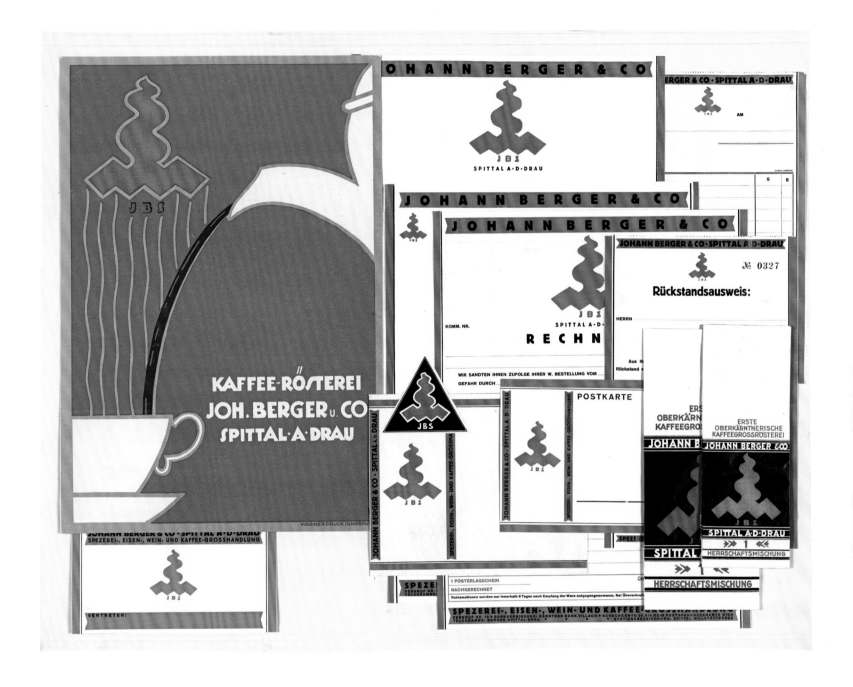

3.
Carl-Ernst Hinkefuss, Packaging
for Kaffee Roesterei Johann
Berger & Co., *c.*1920s.
Collage of invoices, stationery,
and packaging mounted on board.
Print on paper.
42.8 x 55.2 cm (16 ⅞ x 21 ¾ in).

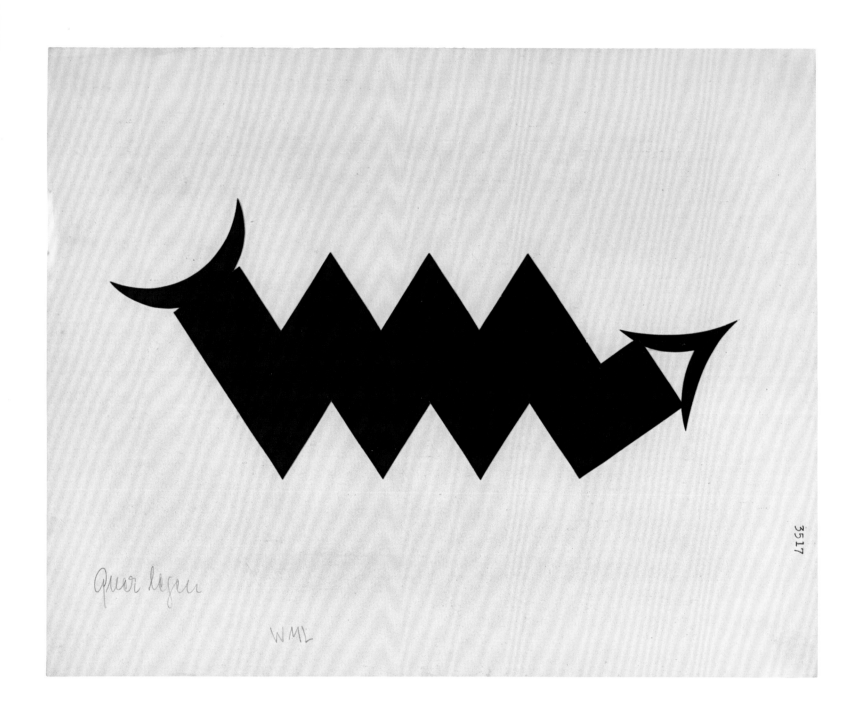

4.
Carl-Ernst Hinkefuss, Logo
"WML", n.d.
Black paper pasted on white
paper.
22.5 x 28.5 cm (8 ⅞ x 11 ¼ in).

5.
Egidio Bonfante, Poster
advertising the Olivetti Lettera 22
portable typewriter, 1951.
Lithograph and photolithograph.
70.5 x 49.5 cm (27 ¾ x 19 ½ in).
The Museum of Modern Art,
New York. Gift of Olivetti S.p.A.

6.
Ing. C. Olivetti & C., Poster advertising "nastri dattilografici (typewriter ribbons) ICO Olivetti", *c.*1950.
Lithograph mounted on canvas.
71.12 x 50.8 cm (28 x 20 in).
San Francisco Museum of Modern Art.

8.
Gyorgy Kepes, "Socrates on Doing Right or Wrong," 1951–2. Advertisement for Container Corporation of America, in the series *Great Ideas of Western Man*.
Print on heavy paper stock.
35.5 x 28.4 cm (14 x 11 ³⁄₁₆ in).

7.
Joseph Hirsch, "Theodore Roosevelt on the Purpose of Government," 1954–6. Advertisement for Container Corporation of America, in the series *Great Ideas of Western Man*.
Print on heavy paper stock.
35.5 x 28.4 cm (14 x 11 ³⁄₁₆ in).

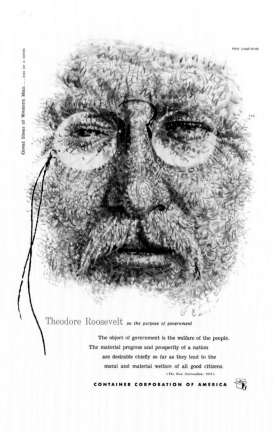

Socrates ON DOING RIGHT OR WRONG

A man who is good for anything ought not to calculate the chance of
living or dying; he ought only to consider whether in doing
anything he is doing right or wrong.... For neither in war
nor yet at law ought I or any man to use every means of
escaping death....The difficulty, my friends, is not to avoid death,
but to avoid unrighteousness....Wherefore, O judges,
be of good cheer about death, and know of a certainty that no evil
can happen to a good man in life or after death.

(From Plato's *Apology*)

CONTAINER CORPORATION OF AMERICA

ARTIST: GYORGY KEPES

9.
Chuck Ax, "Washington on
Foreign Policy," 1954–6.
Advertisement for Container
Corporation of America,
in the series *Great Ideas of
Western Man*.
Print on heavy paper stock.
35.5 x 28.4 cm (14 x 11 3/16 in).

10.
Saul Bass, "John Stuart Mill on
the Pursuit of Truth," 1956–8.
Advertisement for Container
Corporation of America, in the
series *Great Ideas of Western
Man*.
Print on heavy paper stock.
35.5 x 28.4 cm (14 x 11 3/16 in).

John Stuart Mill ON THE PURSUIT OF TRUTH

Not the violent conflict between parts of the truth, but the quiet suppression of half of it, is the formidable evil; there is always hope when people are forced to listen to both sides; it is when they attend only to one that errors harden into prejudices, and truth itself ceases to have the effect of truth, by being exaggerated into falsehood. *(On Liberty, 1856)*

would put an end to the evils of religious or philosophical sectarianism. Every truth which men of narrow capacity are in earnest about, is sure to be asserted, inculcated, and in many ways even acted on, as if no other truth existed in the world, or at all events none that could limit or qualify the first. I acknowledge that the tendency of all opinions to become sectarian is not cured by the freest discussion, but is often heightened and exacerbated thereby; the truth which ought to have been, but was not, seen, being rejected all the more violently because proclaimed by persons regarded as opponents. But it is not on the impassioned partisan, it is on the calmer and more disinterested bystander, that this collision of opinions works its salutary effect. Not the violent conflict between parts of the truth, but the quiet suppression of half of it, is the formidable evil; there is always hope when people are forced to listen to both sides; it is when they attend only to one that errors harden into prejudices, and truth itself ceases to have the effect of truth, by being exaggerated into falsehood. And since there are few mental attributes more rare than that judicial faculty which can sit in intelligent judgment between two sides of a question, of which only one is represented by an advocate before it, truth has no chance but in proportion as every side of it, every opinion which embodies any fraction of the truth, not only finds advocates, but is so advanced as to be listened to. We have now recognised the necessity to the mental well-being of mankind (on which all their other well-being depends) of freedom of opinion, and freedom of the expression of opinion, on four distinct grounds; which we will now briefly recapitulate. First, if any opinion is compelled to silence, that opinion may, for aught we can certainly know, be true. To deny this is to assume our own infallibility. Secondly, though the silenced opinion be an error, it may, and very commonly does, contain a portion of truth; and since the general or prevailing opinion on any subject is rarely or never the whole truth, it is only by the collision of adverse opinions that the remainder of the truth has any chance of

ARTIST: SAUL BASS

CONTAINER CORPORATION OF AMERICA

DESIGN

11.
Designer unknown, Proceedings
of the seventh IDCA conference,
1957.
Print on thin paper stock.
18.4 x 36.8 cm (7 ¼ x 14 ½ in).

12.
Ted Rand and unknown designer,
Report: *Ninth International
Design Conference in Aspen*,
1959.
Print on paper.
22.8 x 30.6 cm (9 x 12 ¹⁄₁₆ in).

13.
James Cross, Poster
announcing the thirteenth
IDCA conference, *Design
and the American Image
Abroad*, 1963.
Print on paper.
53 x 27.9 cm (20 ⅞ x 11 in).

14.
Paul Rand, Announcement of
the sixteenth IDCA conference,
*Sources and Resources of 20th
Century Design*, 1966.
Print on paper.
21.2 x 27.6 cm (8 ⅜ x 10 ⅞ in).

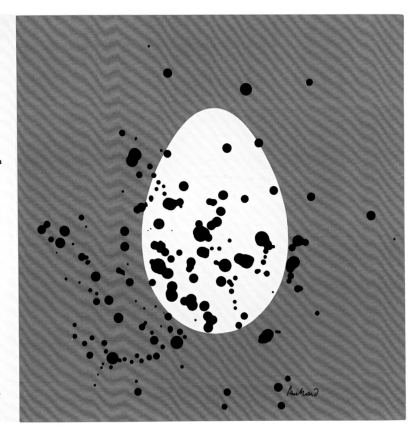

Sources and Resources
of 20th Century Design

June 19 to 24, 1966
The International Design
Conference in Aspen

15.
Designer unknown, Booklet
with speakers' biographies for the
eighteenth IDCA Conference,
1968.
Print on shiny paper stock, paper
and transparent paper. The
photograph printed on the
transparent paper combined with
the photograph on the underlying
paper makes up the complete
image of the speakers.
26.6 x 26.6 cm (10 ½ x 10 ½ in).

Reyner Banham
program chairman
Reyner Banham received his bachelor's degree in history at the Courtauld Institute of Art
University of London, and later received his doctorate there for a thesis which appeared
in book form under the title, "Theory and Design in the First Machine Age." Dr. Banham
is a member of the teaching staff of the Bartlett School of Architecture, University College,
London, and has also served as chairman of the Working-Group on Definition and Doctrine
of the International Council of Societies for Industrial Design.

Morley Markson
designer, film producer and photographer
Morley Markson began his career at Kaiser Aluminum in Chicago, working on geodesic
domes. Later, in private practice, he designed products for Clairtone, National Rubber,
Pneuco Machinery and a number of other companies. Mr. Markson has been an active
photographer for many years and has given a number of one-man shows since 1963.
His design and photographic abilities were demonstrated at Expo '67, where he designed
the International Exhibition of Photography Pavilion and the total physical environment
of the Kaleidoscope Pavilion, including the film, "Man and Color." He was the recipient of
the first Annual Award of the Association of Professional Industrial Designers of Ontario.

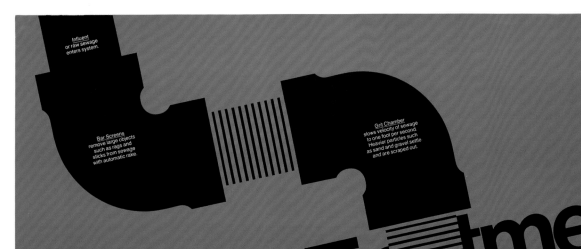

16.
Peter Bradford, "Sewage Treatment," poster designed in conjunction with the twenty-second IDCA conference, *The Invisible City*, 1972. Print on coated paper. 88.1 x 61.2 cm (34 ¹¹⁄₁₆ x 24 ⅛ in).

17.
Designer unknown, Poster announcing the program for the twenty-fourth IDCA conference, *Between Self & System*, 1974. Print on paper. 111.2 x 27.9 cm (43 ¹³⁄₁₆ x 11 in).

18.
Richard Neutra, Participants at the fourth IDCA Conference, 1954, including Brazilian landscape architect Roberto Burle Marx (in center with dark hair and glasses). After their meeting in Aspen, Neutra and Burle Marx collaborated on a few projects.
Crayon on paper.
25 x 34.5 cm (9 ⅞ x 13 ⅝ in).
Courtesy of Dion Neutra, Architect.

Aspen - Burle Marx

453

19.
Richard Neutra, Interior of
conference tent during the
second IDCA conference,
view towards stage, 1952.
Crayon on paper.
25 x 35 cm (9 ⅞ x 13 ¾ in).
Courtesy of Dion Neutra,
Architect.

20.
Lester Beall, logo for Caterpillar,
loose sketchbook page, *c*.1967.
Magic marker on paper.
35.2 x 28 cm (13 ⅞ x 11 1⁄16 in).

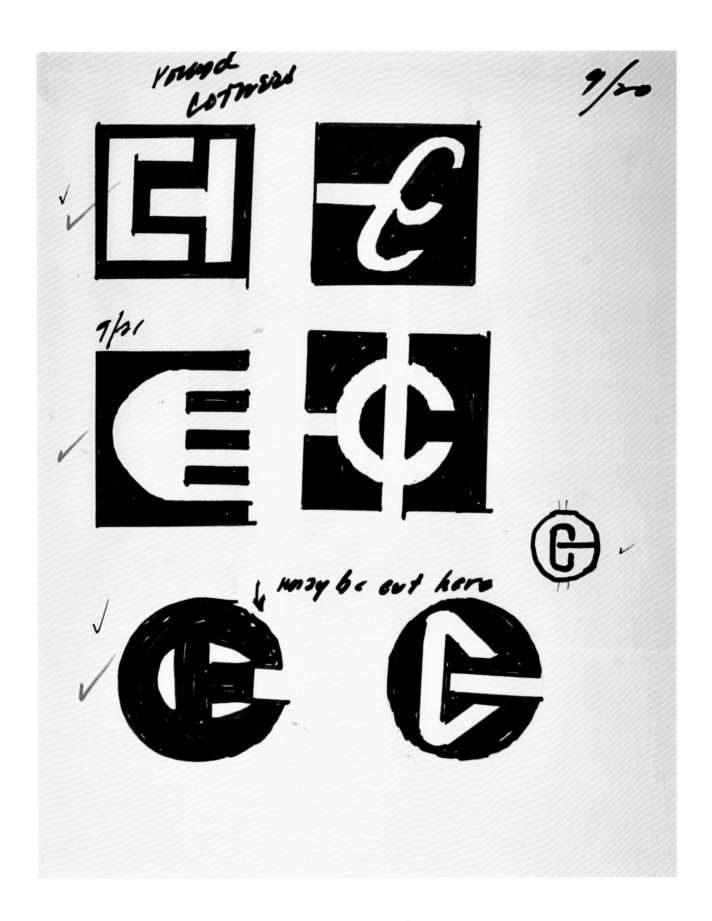

21.
Lester Beall, *Connecticut General Style Book*, 1958.
A style book instructs a company's employees on how to use a logo on letterhead, business cards, and even on buildings.
Print on coated heavy paper.
22.8 x 23.4 cm (9 x 9 ¼ in).

22.
Paul Rand, *Westinghouse
Standard Sign Manual*, 1962.
Print on paper.
27.6 x 42.5 cm (10 ⅞ x 16 ¾ in).

23.
Paul Rand, Poster for
Cummins, Inc., 1973.
Print on paper.
91.4 x 60.9 cm (36 x 24 in).

24.
Will Burtin, sketch design
for a logo for the Upjohn
company, n.d.
Pencil on paper.
20.3 x 12.3 cm (8 x 4 ⅞ in).

Owens Illinois Annual Report '71

25.
Chermayeff & Geismar, *Owens Illinois Annual Report '71*.
Print on paper.
27.9 x 21.5 cm (11 x 8 ½ in).

26.
Chermayeff & Geismar,
Mobil, Corporate Identity 1, poster, late 1960s.
Published by the Mead Library of Ideas, Chicago.
Print on coated paper.
43.1 x 50.8 cm (17 x 20 in).

Mead Library of Ideas presents
the first showing of a
comprehensive corporate
identity program, designed
for Mobil Oil Corporation.
Work from the offices of
Eliott Noyes & Associates,
Chermayeff & Geismar Associates,
Doyle Dane Bernbach
and Fuller, Smith & Ross
will be exhibited.

Corporate Identity 1

Mead Library of Ideas
Forty-first floor
20 North Wacker Drive
Chicago, Illinois
April 24 to May 31
Weekdays 9 am to 5 pm

Design: Chermayeff & Geismar Associates
Paper: Mead Black and White 70 lb. text

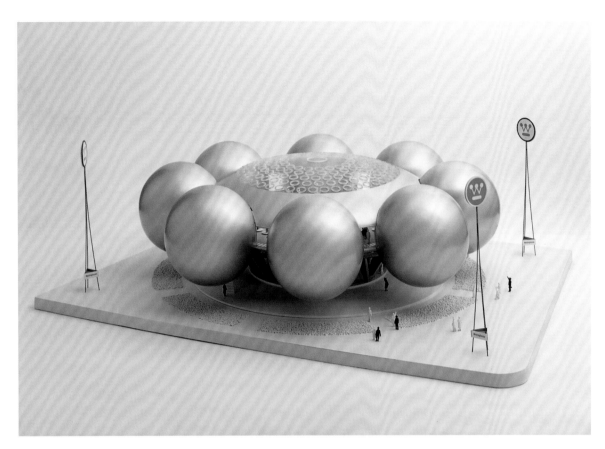

27.
Eliot Noyes, Model for the
Westinghouse Pavilion
at 1964 New York World's
Fair, 1961, not built.
Painted wood, unknown
plastic, and PMMA.
20.32 x 81.28 x 64.14 cm
(8 x 32 x 25 ¼ in).

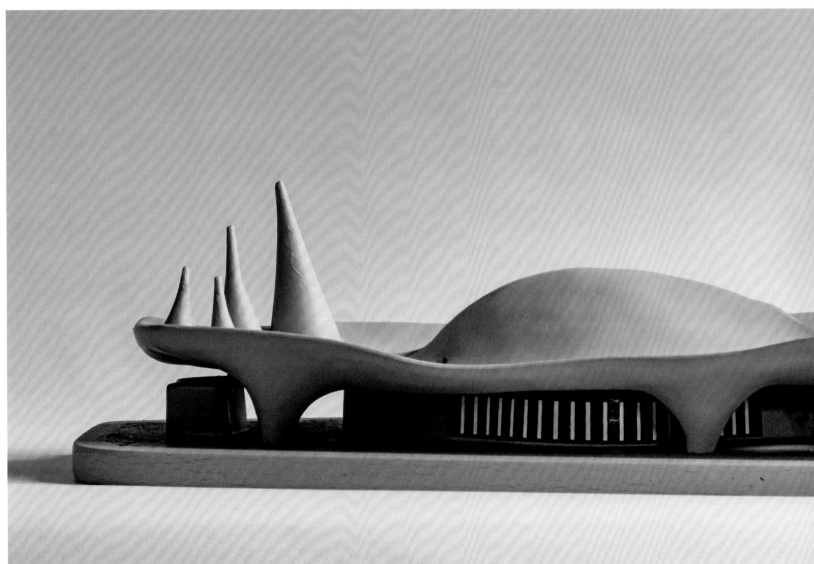

28.
Will Burtin, Model made
by Displaymasters, Inc., for
the Kodak Pavilion at the
1964 New York's Fair,
built. Kodak had several
copies of this model made
and distributed them to
Kodak dealers in order to
create excitement for the
company's participation
at the world's fair.
Painted composition and
plastic; painted plastic
and paper; mounted on a
painted particle-board base.
16.5 x 60.9 x 35.5 cm
(6 ½ x 24 x 14 in).

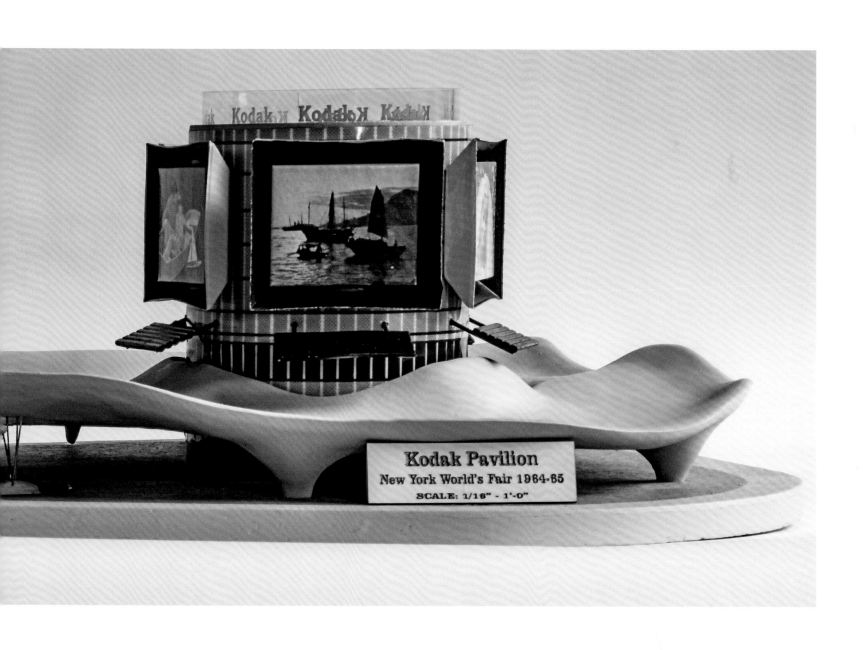

Kodak Pavilion
New York World's Fair 1964-65
SCALE: 1/16" - 1'-0"

29.
Ezra Stoller, Pepsi Cola
Building designed by
Skidmore, Owings & Merrill
architects, New York, NY,
1960.
Ezra Stoller © Esto.

30.
Herbert V. Gosweiler,
Predicta television,
manufactured by Philco
(Philadelphia Storage
Battery Company), 1959.
Metal, glass, plastic.
Overall: 62.2 x 62.5 x
27.3 cm (24 ½ x 24 ⅝ x
10 ¾ in).
Cooper Hewitt, Smithsonian
Design Museum, New York.
Gift of Jan Staller in honor
of Max Staller, 2008-29-1.

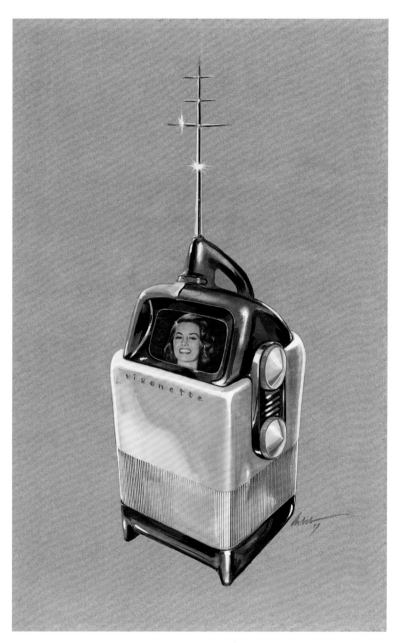

31.
Richard Arbib, Drawing, design for
Visionette Portable Television, 1947.
Brush and watercolor, gouache,
collaged printed image on blue-gray
wove paper.
50.3 x 32.2 cm (19 13/16 x 12 11/16 in).
Cooper Hewitt, Smithsonian Design
Museum, New York. Museum
purchase through the gift of Mrs.
Edward C. Post, 1992-183-7.

32.
Paul Rand, Advertisement, "this
is the new IBM electric", 1960s.
Print on paper.
28 x 20.9 cm (11 1/16 x 8 1/4 in).

33.
Ettore Sottsass and Perry
A. King, Valentine Portable
Typewriter and case for Olivetti,
1969.
Molded ABS plastic, metal,
and rubber.
11.4 x 34.3 x 35.6 cm (4 ½ x
13 ½ x 14 in).
Los Angeles County Museum
of Art, Gift of Daniel Ostroff
(AC1992.293.2a-b).

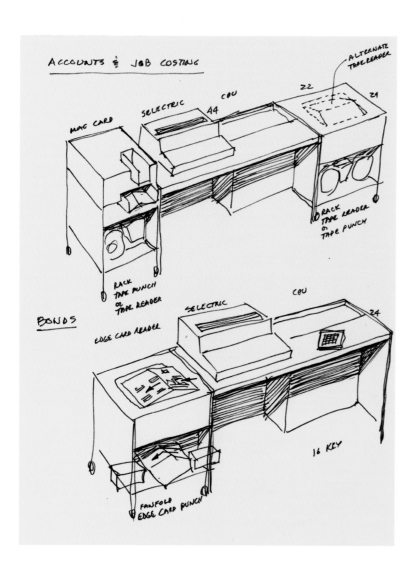

34.
Richard Hollerith, Drawing of magnetic card processor/ Selectric typewriter and CPU integrated in one workstation, "Accounting & Job Costing/Bonds." Ink on paper.
27.6 x 21.2 cm
(10 15/16 x 8 3/8 in.)

35.
Garth Huxtable, Design for a computer workstation for IBM, elevation, c.December 1956.
Crayon on paper.
22.8 x 29.8 cm
(9 x 11 3/4 in).

36.
Henry Dreyfuss, Model
500 telephone, for Bell
Telephone Laboratories,
manufactured by Western
Electric Manufacturing
Company, 1953.
Molded plastic, metal,
and rubber.
12.3 x 21 x 22.7 cm
(4 $^{13}/_{16}$ x 8 $^{1}/_{4}$ x 8 $^{15}/_{16}$ in).
Museum transfer from
Exhibitions Department,
2009-50-1-a/c. Cooper
Hewitt, Smithsonian Design
Museum, New York.

37.
Henry Dreyfuss, Design for single-
lens reflex camera (Wareham),
for Polaroid, 7/12/1963.
Graphite on tracing paper.
23 x 30.3 cm (9 $\frac{1}{16}$ x 11 $\frac{15}{16}$ in).
Cooper Hewitt, Smithsonian
Design Museum, New York. Gift of
Henry Dreyfuss, 1972-88-353.

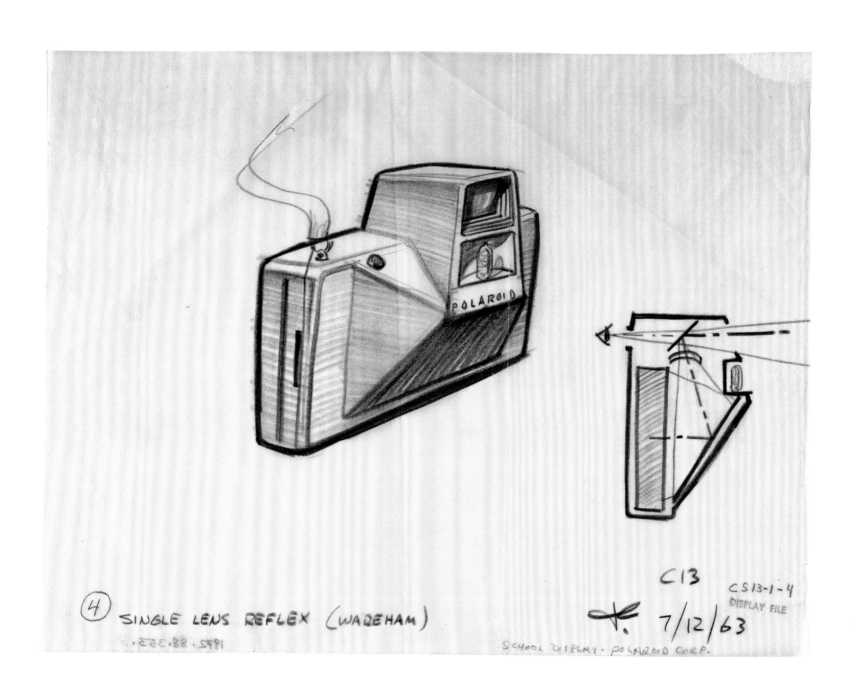

38.
Henry Dreyfuss, Drawing
for box camera #5811,
built-in flash, for Polaroid,
5/12/1965.
Graphite on tracing tissue.
33 x 48.2 cm (13 x 19 in).
Cooper Hewitt, Smithsonian
Design Museum, New York.
Gift of Henry Dreyfuss, 1972-
88-356.

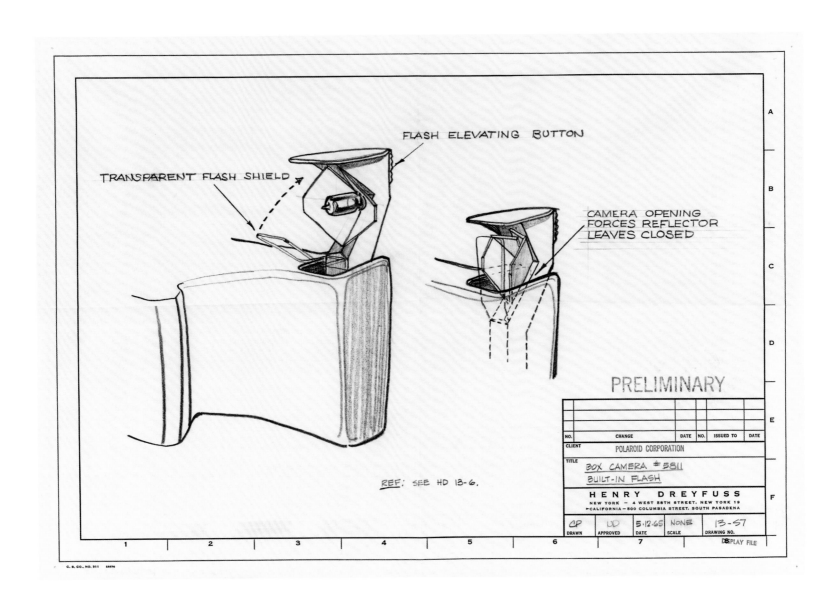

39.
Charles and Ray Eames,
DSS plastic stacking chair
with table arm, 1960–1.
Fiberglass, steel, plastic
laminate, wood, and nylon.
62.2 x 49.5 x 81.3 cm
(24 ½ x 19 ½ x 32 in).
Los Angeles County Museum
of Art, Los Angeles. Gift of
the employees of Herman
Miller, Inc. (M.89.104.3).

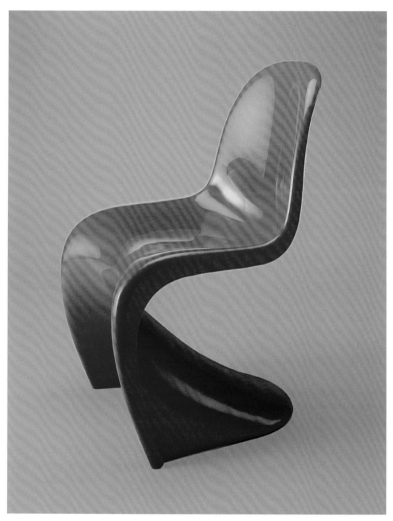

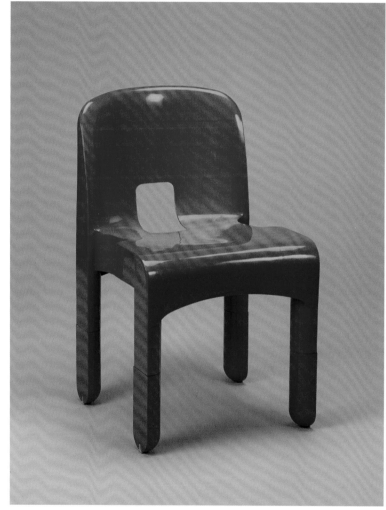

40.
Verner Panton, Panton Chair
for Herman Miller Furniture
Company, 1968.
Molded plastic.
48.3 x 44.5 x 83.2 cm (19 x
17 ½ x 32 ¾ in).
Los Angeles County Museum
of Art, Los Angeles. Gift of
the employees of Herman
Miller, Inc. (M.89.104.13).

41.
Joe Colombo, 4860 side
chair, c.1965. Manufactured
by Kartell S.p.A in Milan,
Italy.
Injection-molded ABS plastic,
rubber.
72 x 43.3 x 43 cm (28 ⅜
x 17 ¹⁄₁₆ x 16 ¹⁵⁄₁₆ in).
Cooper Hewitt, Smithsonian
Design Museum, New York.
Gift of Dr. Herbert Appel,
1986-115-1.

42.
Poul Kjaerholm, PK 24
Chaise Longue, for
Christensen/Herman Miller,
1965.
Stainless steel, leather
and cane.
87 x 155 x 67 cm (34 ¼
x 61 x 26 ⅜ in).
The Museum of Modern Art,
New York. Gift of Michael
Maharam.

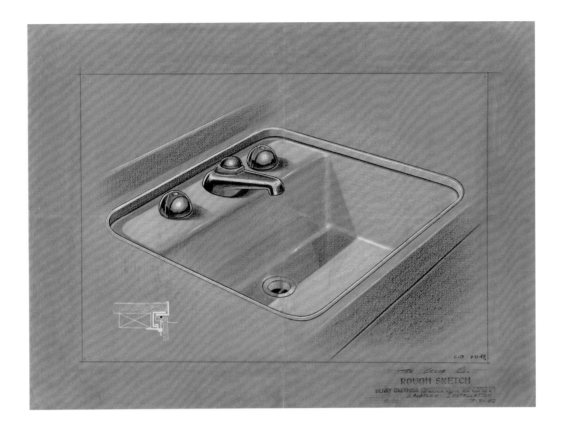

43.
Henry Dreyfuss, Drawing, Lavatory Installation: Sink for Crane Co., March 31, 1949.
Charcoal, white chalk, and graphite on heavy gray paper.
37.3 x 50.2 cm (14 ¹¹⁄₁₆ x 19 ¾ in).
Cooper Hewitt, Smithsonian Design Museum, New York. Gift of Henry Dreyfuss, 1972-88-335.

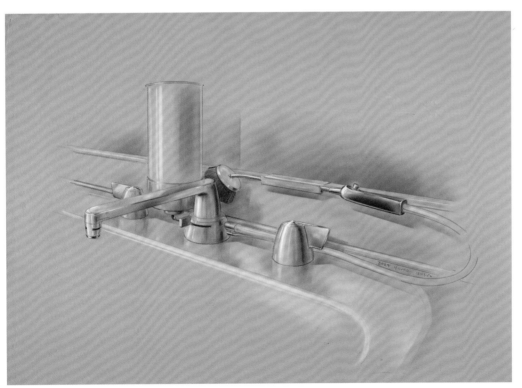

44.
Donald Deskey, Drawing, detergent dispenser, dish brush, and faucet, December 13, 1956.
Graphite and pastel on paper.
49.7 x 64.2 cm (19 ⁹⁄₁₆ x 25 ¼ in).
Cooper Hewitt, Smithsonian Design Museum, New York. Gift of Donald Deskey, 1988-101-1528.

45.
N.N., Blender for Hollywood Liquifier Corporation, Glendale, CA, c.1950.
Molded plastic, glass, metal, metal wire.
Overall, not incl. cord: 37.3 x 20.2 x 15.2 cm (14 ¹¹⁄₁₆ x 7 ¹⁵⁄₁₆ x 6 in).
Cooper Hewitt, Smithsonian Design Museum, New York. Museum purchase from Decorative Arts Association Acquisition Fund, 1993-150-2-a/c.

46.
Peter Schlumbohm, Chemex
coffee maker for Chemex
Corp., 1941.
Pyrex glass, wood, and
leather.
Height 24.13 cm (9 ½ in),
diameter 15.5 cm (6 ⅛ in).
The Museum of Modern Art,
New York. Gift of Lewis &
Conger (51.1943).

47.
N.N., Atomic espresso maker, patented by Brevetti Robbiati, 1950s. Aluminum, brass, plastic, and Bakelite.
Overall: 22.5 x 21.2 x 21 cm (8 ⅞ x 8 ⅜ x 8 ¼ in).
Cooper Hewitt, Smithsonian Design Museum, New York. Museum purchase through gift of Neil Sellin, 1999-3-1-a/e.

48.
Barnes and Reinecke, for
Wear-Ever Aluminum Inc.,
Juicer, perspective
view, #1033, JM, *c.*1954.
Graphite and crayon on
tracing paper.
42.8 x 34.8 cm (16 ⁷⁄₈ x
13 ¹⁵⁄₁₆ in.)

49.
Thomas Lamb, "Reversible
Wedge Studies, Paint Brush
Handles," 1949–50.
Graphite, ink, and crayon
on vellum.
28 x 21.5 cm (11 x 8 ⁷⁄₁₆ in.)

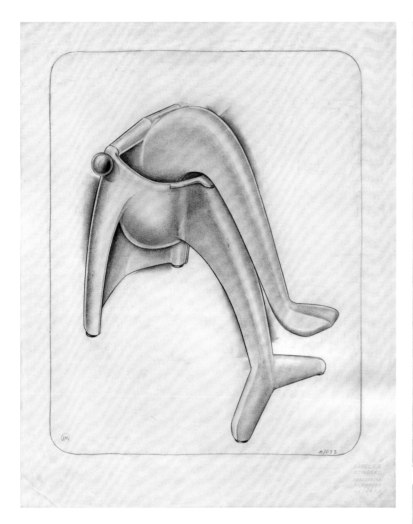

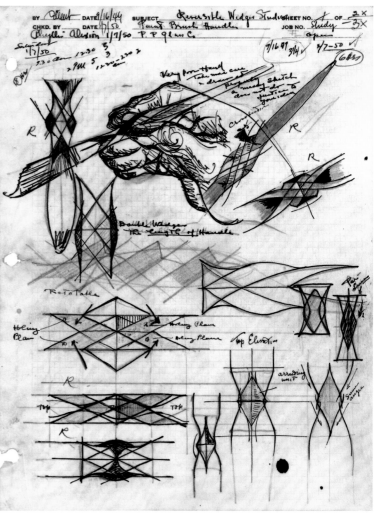

50.
Garth Huxtable, Design for
a Millers Falls drill, view from
the side, n.d.
Pencil, color pencil, and
crayon on vellum mounted on
board.
22.2 x 29 cm (8 ¾ x 11 ⁷⁄₁₆ in).

BIOGRAPHIES OF MAJOR DESIGNERS REPRESENTED IN THE EXHIBITION *CREATIVITY ON THE LINE*

SELINA HER

RICHARD ARBIB
(USA, 1917–95)

Arbib was an industrial designer who designed functional as well as fanciful everyday products. His clients included the Hamilton Watch Company, Argus Cameras, and Republic Aircraft. Throughout his life, Arbib worked on a diverse array of objects, from yachts to vacuum cleaners to airplanes. He also was well known as an innovative car designer.
Michael Elliott, "Richard H. Arbib, 77, Designer of Array of Consumer Products," *New York Times*, March 3, 1995, www.nytimes.com/1995/03/03/obituaries/richard-h-arbib-77-designer-of-array-of-consumer-products.html.

SAUL BASS
(USA, 1920–96)

Bass received his training under Gyorgy Kepes at Brooklyn College, New York. After his move to Los Angeles in 1946, he began a distinguished graphic design career in advertising for the movie industry. He became best known for his designs of title sequences and posters for such major movies as *The Seven Year Itch* (1955), *The Man with the Golden Arm* (1955), *Vertigo* (1958) and *Psycho* (1960). He also created corporate identities for many corporations, including AT&T, United Airlines, and Warner Communications.
Peter Dormer, *The Illustrated Dictionary of Twentieth Century Designers* (London: Quarto, 1991), pp.50–1.
Jennifer Bass and Pat Kirkham, *Saul Bass: a Life in Film and Design* (London: Laurence King, 2011).

HERBERT BAYER
(Austria, 1900–85, USA)

Starting in 1920, Bayer studied for four years at the Bauhaus in Weimar with Wassily Kandinsky and László Moholy-Nagy, among others. He in turn became a teacher there in 1925, directing the typography and advertising workshop. During that time, he developed an experimental universal typeface without conventional capital or lower-case letters. Bayer came to the United States in 1938 and was asked to design both the exhibition and the accompanying book *Bauhaus 1919–1928*

at the Museum of Modern Art. From 1946 onwards, he was a consultant for the Container Corporation of America, assisting its president, Walter Paepcke, with his many projects in Aspen, Colorado.
Modern Art in Advertising, Designs for Container Corporation of America (Chicago: Paul Theobald, 1946), ills 2–12.
Peter Dormer, *The Illustrated Dictionary of Twentieth Century Designers* (London: Quarto, 1991), p.52.

LESTER BEALL
(USA, 1903–69)

Beall was a graphic and industrial designer known for his posters for the Rural Electrification Administration as well as for his corporate identity work. Born in Missouri and trained in engineering and art history at Chicago's Lane Technical School and the University of Chicago, his career intertwined the precise and disciplined with creative expression. Inspired by European modernism, he developed his own unique style using flat abstract shapes, directional arrows, woodcuts, and popping typography while restricting himself to a limited color palette. MoMA New York granted him a solo exhibition in 1937, making him the first commercial designer to receive that honor and propelling him to success. Some of the corporations for which he worked in the post-World War II era were Caterpillar, Connecticut General, and International Paper.
Peter Dormer, *The Illustrated Dictionary of Twentieth Century Designers* (London: Quarto, 1991), pp.52–3.
R. Roger Remington, *Nine Pioneers in American Graphic Design* (Cambridge, MA: MIT Press, 1989).
R. Roger Remington, *Lester Beall: Trailblazer of American Graphic Design* (New York, W. W. Norton, 1996).

EGIDIO BONFANTE
(Italy, 1922–2004)

Trained as an artist and architect in Milan, Bonfante's career changed dramatically in 1948 when he met Adriano Olivetti and was hired to work for the latter's office

equipment manufacturing company. He not only designed publications and posters for Olivetti, but also trade fair pavilions, showrooms, and exhibitions. He continued to work for this enterprise until the 1980s. Some scholars have suggested that Bonfante may have been the first to use the Helvetica typeface in Italy in 1960 on the cover of the Olivetti-supported publication *Comunità*.
"Egidio Bonfante," www.olivettiani.org/egidio-bonfante.html.
"Massimo Vignelli," *Design Culture* (n.p., n.d.), www.designculture.it/interview/massimo-vignelli.html.

WILL BURTIN
(Germany, 1908–72, USA)

Burtin studied typesetting and graphic design in Germany and set up his studio in Cologne in 1927. When the Nazis announced that they wanted him to work for them, he left Germany and arrived in the United States in 1939. During the war, Burtin first taught in New York and when called up into the army, he designed gunnery manuals for the US Air Force. His role as art director of *Fortune* magazine (1945–9) helped elevate that publication's status in America. Burtin is notable for his pursuit to bridge science and art, and for clarifying complex subjects in these fields to the general public. He did this through 2D media as exemplified in *Scope*, a physicians' magazine published by the Upjohn Company that presented scientific data in innovative ways. More dramatically, Burtin created educational exhibitions like giant models of the human brain or a human cell that brought science to life in a tangible way. In addition to the Upjohn Company, some of Burtin's other clients were Eastman Kodak and Herman Miller Furniture.
Peter Dormer, *The Illustrated Dictionary of Twentieth Century Designers* (London: Quarto, 1991), p.64.
R. Roger Remington, *Nine Pioneers in American Graphic Design* (Cambridge, MA: MIT Press, 1989).
R. Roger Remington, and Robert S. Fripp, *Design and Science: The Life and Work of Will Burtin* (Aldershot, Hampshire, and Burlington, VT: Lund Humphries, 2007).

JEAN CARLU
(France, 1900–97)

After an accident cost him his right arm at age 18, Carlu turned from following in the footsteps of his architect family toward graphic design. He subsequently worked in advertising most of his life. Having been sent to the United States to work on the French pavilion at the 1939 World's Fair in New York, Carlu stayed there until 1953. During World War II, he worked as the chief of the Graphic Division of the French Ministry of Information. Through his posters he promoted the efforts of France and the USA in the Allied war effort. He designed several advertisements for the Container Corporation of America.
Modern Art in Advertising, Designs for Container Corporation of America (Chicago: Paul Theobald, 1946), ills 15–18.
"Jean Carlu," *Smithsonian American Art Museum*, Smithsonian Institution (n.d.), http://americanart.si.edu/search/artist_bio.cfm?ID=749.
"Jean Carlu," *RoGallery* (n.d.), http://rogallery.com/Carlu/Carlu-bio.htm.

CHERMAYEFF & GEISMAR

Founded in 1957, the office of Chermayeff & Geismar has been a major player in the design world. The firm has clients not only in the US, but also in Europe, Asia, Latin America, and the Middle East. Its expertise in graphic design has translated into branding, motion graphics, and exhibitions, including an installation at the Ellis Island Immigration Museum. Now known as Chermayeff & Geismar & Haviv, the firm has undergone several iterations since its inception, but throughout has maintained a process emphasizing collaboration and attention to detail. Principal Ivan Chermayeff (b. 1932) is the son of architect Serge Chermayeff. Together with his partner Tom Geismar (b. 1931), Ivan Chermayeff received many awards, including the AIGA Medal for 1979.
"About the Firm," *Chermayeff & Geismar & Haviv* (n.d.), http://www.cghnyc.com/the-firm/.

JOE COLOMBO
(Italy, 1930–71)

Colombo's training included the study of painting at the Accademia di Belle Arti di Brera and architecture at the Politecnico, both in Milan. However, he pursued a career in neither field and instead began to work around 1955 as an industrial designer. Colombo was very interested in the use of new materials and technologies, such as plastic injection molding. He also was intrigued by the design of compactly organized storage or kitchen units, as evidenced by his Portable Storage System (1969), and his Kitchen Box (1963), which contained a refrigerator, stove, oven, chopping block, and drawers for kitchen tools.
Joe C. Colombo, Charles Eames, Fritz Eichler, Verner Panton, Roger Tallon, qu'est ce que le design?, exh. cat. (Paris: Centre de création industrielle, 1969).
Peter Dormer, *The Illustrated Dictionary of Twentieth Century Designers* (London: Quarto, 1991), p.77.

DONALD DESKEY
(USA, 1894–1989)

Deskey was an industrial designer who had studied architecture at the University of California, Berkeley, and painting at the School of the Art Institute of Chicago and the Art Students League in New York, among other places. He was strongly influenced by the 1925 International Exposition of Modern Decorative and Industrial Arts in Paris, and by the style promoted by that fair. Deskey went on to design furniture, lighting, and packaging. He developed Weldtex, a striated wood laminate, which is still used today.
"Donald Deskey," *Art Directory*, Ketterer Kunst (n.d.), www.donald-deskey.com.

HENRY DREYFUSS
(USA, 1903–72)

Dreyfuss started off as a stage-set designer, and during the 1920s worked with Norman Bel Geddes on Broadway. He opened his own office for stage and industrial design in 1929. He was able to attract important clients, including Bell Laboratories, John Deere, General Electric, the Hoover Company, and the New York Central Rail Road. His AT&T model 500 desk telephone and the Mercury locomotive are some of his most famous designs. In the 1950s, Dreyfuss began to disseminate his design philosophy in writing, especially in his seminal works *Designing For People* (1955) and *The Measure of Man: human factors in design* (1967), in which he promoted the concept of ergonomics in design.
Peter Dormer, *The Illustrated Dictionary of Twentieth Century Designers* (London: Quarto, 1991), pp.85–6.
Russell Flinchum, *Henry Dreyfuss, Industrial Designer: The Man in the Brown Suit* (New York: Cooper-Hewitt National Design Museum and Rizzoli, 1997).

CHARLES AND RAY EAMES
(USA, 1907–78)

Charles Eames was an influential architect and furniture designer well known for his use of new malleable materials, such as plywood, fiberglass, and aluminum. Eames received his earliest architectural training at Washington University in his native St. Louis. He did not stay at that school for more than two years, at which point he opened his own office in that city. In 1938, he moved to Bloomfield Hills, Michigan, to attend the Cranbrook Academy of Art first as a student and later as the head of the Industrial Design Department. Here he met Eero Saarinen, with whom he participated in the "Organic Design in Home Furnishings" competition organized by MoMA New York (1940–1). Their molded plywood chair won the first prize. At Cranbrook, Charles also met Ray Kaiser, whom he married in 1941, and with whom he moved to Los Angeles that same year. There, Charles and Ray began a practice in which responsibility for the creation of most major projects was shared by both of them. They designed numerous chairs and other pieces of furniture, exhibitions, films and slide shows, and toys. Their house in Pacific Palisades, California, counts among the most innovative houses designed in the second half of the twentieth century.
Peter Dormer, *The Illustrated Dictionary of Twentieth Century Designers* (London: Quarto, 1991), p.89.

Pat Kirkham, *Charles and Ray Eames: Designers of the Twentieth Century* (Cambridge, MA.: MIT Press, 1995).
Donald Albrecht (ed.), *The Work of Charles and Ray Eames: A Legacy of Invention* (New York: Harry N. Abrams, Inc., in association with the Library of Congress and the Vitra Design Museum, 1997).

HERBERT GOSWEILER
(USA, 1915–91)
Gosweiler was one of the leaders, along with Severin Jonassen, of a design team at Philco, the Philadelphia Storage Battery Company. Among the objects he helped create was the futuristic Predicta Television, made in 1959. The creation of the Predicta line was ultimately unsuccessful as its design was too far out of the public's comfort zone. In addition, the prototypes and concepts for the Predicta Televisions used advanced technology like injection molding not yet available for consumer-manufactured goods.

Gail Davidson, "The Future of Television," *Cooper Hewitt*, Smithsonian Design Museum, August 16, 2015, www.cooperhewitt.org/2015/08/16/the-future-of-television.

HANS GUGELOT
(Netherlands Indies (now Indonesia), 1920–65, Germany)
Gugelot studied at the ETH in Zurich and after his graduation in 1946 worked in the office of the Swiss artist Max Bill, who was also one of the founders in 1953 of the School of Design in Ulm (Hochschule für Gestaltung Ulm). In 1954 he moved to Frankfurt to work as a designer for Braun and teach in Ulm. Together with his colleague Dieter Rams, Gugelot advocated a functional design method, which eschewed ornamentation, and promoted the idea that design was an integral part of an industrial product, not a pretty wrapping around the engineer-produced core.

Peter Dormer, *The Illustrated Dictionary of Twentieth Century Designers* (London: Quarto, 1991), p.110.

RICHARD HOLLERITH
(USA, b. 1926)
Hollerith studied Naval Science and Geology at Dartmouth University as well as industrial design at the University of the Arts (then the Philadelphia Museum School of Art). Before starting on his own, he worked for the Monroe Calculating Machine Company (1954–6) and was an account manager for Henry Dreyfuss Associates (1956–66). Much of his design work is in the realm of office products, business equipment, and computer workstations. He is the grandson of Herman Hollerith (1860–1929), the inventor of the punch-card system.

"Richard Hollerith Jr., FIDSA," *Industrial Designers Society of America*, January 8, 2010, www.idsa.org/content/richard-hollerith-jr-fidsa.
"Biographical Sketch," Richard Hollerith Papers, Accession 2054, Hagley Museum and Library, available via findingaids.hagley.org/xtf/.

L. GARTH HUXTABLE
(USA, 1911–89)
Huxtable studied at the Massachusetts School of Art and worked with such industrial design luminaries as Norman Bel Geddes, for whom, among many other designs, he worked on the General Motors Futurama display at the New York World's Fair (1939), and Henry Dreyfuss. He opened his own office soon after the end of World War II. Together with his wife, Ada Louise Huxtable, who would later become famous as the architecture critic of the *New York Times*, he designed the china and silverware for the Four Seasons restaurant in New York (1958). He was also involved in the design of dinnerware for the New York restaurant La Fonda del Sol (1960), which became famous for its colorful Alexander Girard interiors. In addition, he designed power tools for Millers Falls for more than 20 years.

John Pile, *Dictionary of 20th-Century Design* (n.p.: John Pile and Roundtable, 1990), p.124.
Randy Roeder, "L. Garth Huxtable: Industrial Designer for Millers Falls," *The Gristmill: The Journal of the Mid-West Tools Collectors Association* (2002).

L. Garth Huxtable Papers, Special Collections, Getty Research Institute, http://archives2.getty.edu:8082/xtf/view?docId=ead/2013.M.2/2013.M.2.xml;chunk.id=ref4;brand=default.

MARSHALL JOHNSON
(USA, b. 1938)
Johnson studied Industrial Design and Art Education at the Rhode Island School of Design, where he graduated in 1960. For the next seven years he worked for Black and Decker, which company hired him as their first in-house designer. In 1967, he joined the Aluminum Company of America (ALCOA), where he created diverse objects using aluminum, including kitchen appliances and furniture; he also designed an oceanographic ship, the ALCOA *Seaprobe*. Four years later he was transferred to ALCOA's aluminum cookware subsidiary, Wear-Ever Industries, Inc., where he stayed until his retirement in 2001.

"Marshall Johnson," *Industrial Designers Society of America*, October 26, 2011, www.idsa.org/members/marshall-johnson.
"Historical Note," Marshall Johnson collection of cookware and appliance design drawings, Accession 2268II, Hagley Museum and Library, available via findingaids.hagley.org/xtf/.

GYORGY KEPES
(Hungary, 1906–2001, USA)
Kepes was an educator and writer on the subject of design. Among the places at which he taught were the New Bauhaus/Institute of Design in Chicago (1937–43) and MIT (1946–74). Notable writings include his book *Language of Vision* (1944), which helped disseminate major Bauhaus ideals, *The New Landscape in Art and Science* (1956), and the *Vision + Value* series, a collection of design-related anthologies. Kepes was greatly influenced by his countryman László Moholy-Nagy, in whose Berlin studio he worked in the early 1930s and through whom he met leading avant-garde artists. He moved with Moholy-Nagy to London in 1936, and then a year later followed the famous artist to Chicago to teach classes in light and color at the New Bauhaus. In that city, he also worked for the Container Corporation of America designing several of

its advertisements. At MIT, Kepes taught visual design, and in the 1960s founded the Center for Advanced Visual Studies.
Modern Art in Advertising, Designs for Container Corporation of America (Chicago, Paul Theobald, 1946), ill.44.
John Pile, *Dictionary of 20th-Century Design* (n.p.: John Pile and Roundtable, 1990), p.138.
Peter Dormer, *The Illustrated Dictionary of Twentieth Century Designers* (London: Quarto, 1991), p.132.

PERRY KING
(UK, b.1938)
King received his training at Birmingham College of Art and moved to Italy in 1964 where a year later he became a design consultant at Olivetti. There, he worked on a wide range of products, including furniture and office machinery, and most famously the Valentine typewriter, which he designed with Ettore Sottsass in 1969. In 1978 he and Santiago Miranda founded King & Miranda, a Milan-based design and architecture firm. They have created office furniture, light fixtures, typefaces, and interior designs.
Peter Dormer, *The Illustrated Dictionary of Twentieth Century Designers* (London: Quarto, 1991), p.134.

POUL KJAERHOLM
(Denmark, 1929–80)
Kjaerholm was a pioneer in cutting-edge Danish furniture design, known for his elegant usage of metal, wood, marble, and plastic. His designs combined the sharpness of geometric shapes with the soft texture of natural materials. They were produced by Fritz Hansen, E. Kold Christensen, and P. P. Furniture. PK 24, also known as the Hammock Chair, which he created in 1965, is perhaps his most famous piece. Kjaerholm was trained at the School of Arts and Crafts in Copenhagen, and lectured there between 1952 and 1956.
John Pile, *Dictionary of 20th-Century Design* (n.p.: John Pile and Roundtable, 1990), p.139.

THOMAS LAMB
(USA, 1897–1988)
Lamb studied at the Art Students League of New York and at Columbia University. He also at a very young age took lessons in anatomy and medical drawing. After initially having worked as an illustrator of children's books and as a textile designer, he took on industrial design. He became best known for his specialty in creating ergonomic handles such as the Wedge-Lock Handle. In fact, after an exhibition at MoMA New York, he became known as the "Handle Man." Allowing for easy and safe use, thanks to his intensive study of the human hand's physiology and its range of movements, Lamb's handles were used in all kinds of equipment, varying from surgical tools to utensils made by Cutco, ALCOA, Skil, and Wear-Ever.
John Pile, *Dictionary of 20th-Century Design* (n.p.: John Pile and Roundtable, 1990), pp.145–6.
"Biographical Sketch," Thomas Lamb Papers, Accession 2181, Hagley Museum and Library, available via findingaids.hagley.org/xtf/.

DOROTHY LIEBES
(USA, 1899–1972)
Liebes' education was primarily academic, as opposed to the trade-oriented training most other designers received. She studied education, anthropology, and art at San Jose State Teachers College and the University of California, Berkeley. It was, nonetheless, during her college time that a teacher first encouraged her to try weaving, which she did and liked. It would still take her several years before she decided to pursue a full-time career in textile design. In 1934, she opened Dorothy Liebes Inc., in San Francisco. Thanks to the success of her work, she became a design consultant to big corporations such as DuPont, Dow, and Bigelow-Sanford, working with chemists, engineers, and technicians, and testing their synthetic fibers through use in her weavings. In addition to these accomplishments, she was Director of Decorative Arts for the 1939 San Francisco World's Fair .
"Dorothy Liebes Papers," *Archives of American Art* (n.d.), www.aaa.si.edu/collections/dorothy-liebes-papers-9143/more.

Regina Lee Blaszczyk, "Designing Synthetics, Promoting Brands: Dorothy Liebes, DuPont Fibres and Post-war American Interiors," *Journal of Design History* 21, issue 1 (2008), pp.75–99.

LEO LIONNI
(The Netherlands, 1910–99, Italy)
Lionni's academic training was in economics, but a childhood love of teaching himself to draw in Amsterdam's museums eventually led to a flourishing artistic career. Now principally renowned as an author and illustrator of numerous highly acclaimed children's books, Lionni launched a career in graphic design in the 1930s, first in Italy and from 1939–60 in the United States. He held a number of high-level positions in this field, including that of design director for Olivetti USA and art director for *Fortune.*
Leo Lionni, *Between Worlds: the autobiography of Leo Lionni* (New York: Knopf, 1997).
"Leo Lionni's Biography," *Scholastic Teachers* (n.p., n.d.), www.scholastic.com/teachers/contributor/leo-lionni.

HERBERT MATTER
(Switzerland, 1907–84, USA)
Early in his career, Matter was greatly influenced by design legends such as A. M. Cassandre, Le Corbusier, Fernand Léger, El Lissitzky, and Man Ray, from whom he synthesized a bit of everything into his own intense yet geometrically rational style. His work spans typography, photography, architecture, and even cinematography. He designed posters for the Container Corporation of America and consulted at Knoll between 1944 and 1956. He joined Yale University's faculty in 1952, first as visiting critic and later as a professor of photography and graphic design.
Modern Art in Advertising, Designs for Container Corporation of America (Chicago: Paul Theobald, 1946), ills 61–8.
Steven Heller and David R. Brown, "Biography," *Herbert Matter* (n.d.), http://herbertmatter.org/welcome/biography.

MARCELLO NIZZOLI
(Italy, 1887–1969)

Nizzoli was a graphic designer, product designer, architect, and painter well versed in diverse styles, and was early on especially influenced by Futurism. He worked for firms like Olivetti, a manufacturer of office machines, and the Necchi Sewing Machine Company, combining organic forms with functionality. Some of his best-known designs are the Lexikon 80 typewriter (1948) and the Lettera 22 portable typewriter (1949–50), both for Olivetti.

"Marcello Nizzoli Biography," *Marcello Nizzoli* (n.p., n.d.), www.marcello-nizzoli.com.
"Marcello Nizzoli," *The Museum of Modern Art* (n.p., n.d.), www.moma.org/collection/artists/4316?locale=en.

ELIOT NOYES
(USA, 1910–77)

Noyes first was trained as an architect at Harvard, where he discovered the Bauhaus through Marcel Breuer and Walter Gropius. He became the director of industrial design at MoMA in New York in 1939 and with some interruptions continued to work there until 1946. Subsequently, Noyes worked for a short time as a design director for Norman Bel Geddes and in 1947 opened his own office for architectural and industrial design. His most important client was IBM, for which company he designed the corporate identity and by-now-famous products, including the 1961 Selectric typewriter. Noyes' firm worked for many other major corporations, such as Xerox, Westinghouse, and Mobil. In addition to visual identities, he also designed physical spaces, like Mobil's gasoline stations with disk-shaped canopies. As president of the International Design Conference in Aspen (IDCA), Noyes championed ethical and aesthetic concerns over commercial ones.

John Pile, *Dictionary of 20th-Century Design* (n.p.: John Pile and Roundtable, 1990), p.189.
Peter Dormer, *The Illustrated Dictionary of Twentieth Century Designers* (London: Quarto, 1991), p.174.
Gordon Bruce, *Eliot Noyes* (London, Phaidon Press, 2006).

VERNER PANTON
(Denmark, 1926–98)

Although he was trained as an architect at the Royal Danish Academy of Fine Arts in Copenhagen and worked for a few years for the architectural firm of Arne Jacobsen, Panton became best known for his designs of chairs, which exhibit the vibrant colors of 1960s pop culture as well as modern technological innovations such as the use of plastic and fiberglass. He created several chairs out of one piece and without legs, the most famous of which is the cantilevered fiberglass and plastic Panton Chair (1968).

Joe C. Colombo, Charles Eames, Fritz Eichler, Verner Panton, Roger Tallon, qu'est ce que le design?, exh. cat. (Paris: Centre de création industrielle, 1969).
Peter Dormer, *The Illustrated Dictionary of Twentieth Century Designers* (London: Quarto, 1991), p.178.

DIETER RAMS
(Germany, b. 1932)

After an education in architecture and interior design and a few years of work in a Frankfurt architect's office, Rams was hired in 1955 as an architect and interior designer by the Braun electrical appliance manufacturing company. He became the company's chief design officer in 1961 and stayed on in that job until 1995. Many Braun products designed by Rams are now household names, such as "Snow White's Coffin" (the SK4 record player). They reflect his personality: exacting and particular, yet clearly successful. Rams' German aesthetic was in tension with the also influential Italian school of design. While some of his ideas on the subject of designing for human needs were similar to those of Ettore Sottsass, Rams ostensibly took on an absolutist definition of good design that the latter rejected. In any case, it is undeniable that his principles of good design have made a significant impact on today's generations, in industrial as well as digital products. Rams also taught at the School of Design in Ulm (Hochschule für Gestaltung Ulm), which is generally considered to have continued the educational principles of the Bauhaus in Germany.

Peter Dormer, *The Illustrated Dictionary of Twentieth Century Designers* (London: Quarto, 1991), p.193.
Sophie Lovell, *Dieter Rams: As Little Design as Possible* (London and New York: Phaidon, 2011).

PAUL RAND
(USA, 1914–96)

Rand grew up in New York, where he studied at Parsons School of Design and the Pratt Institute, as well as the Art Students League. He pioneered new interpretations of the magazine medium, promoting a dynamic use of typography, layout, color, texture, and montage at *Esquire* and *Apparel Arts*. Rand's style was influenced by a mixture of European and American aesthetics, which he applied over the middle decades of the century as he transitioned into corporate identity work. In addition to serving as a consultant with IBM, Westinghouse, and the American Broadcasting Company (ABC), Rand taught at Yale University almost continuously from 1956 to 1985. He also wrote several books, including *Thoughts on Design* (1947), which includes essays on advertising design principles illustrated with his own work.

Peter Dormer, *The Illustrated Dictionary of Twentieth Century Designers* (London: Quarto, 1991), p.191.

JEAN O. REINECKE
(USA, 1909–87)

Reinecke received his art training at Washington University's Art School. He moved to Chicago to work on the Century of Progress exhibition of 1933–4. At the end of the fair, Reinecke decided to stay there and, along with James Barnes as sales manager, he founded the office of Barnes & Reinecke. Their product design and engineering firm grew to have over 400 employees by 1948. In that year, Reinecke left the firm to begin J. O. Reinecke & Associates. There, clients included Caterpillar, Johnson and Johnson, Westinghouse and 3M. For the latter company he designed the Decor Dispenser Model C-15 in 1961, which was available in many different colors and has been in production ever since.

"Jean Otis Reinecke, FIDSA," *Industrial Designers Society of America*, 26 April 2010, www.idsa.org/content/jean-otis-reinecke-fidsa.

EERO SAARINEN
(Finland, 1910–61, USA)
Son of the famous architect Eliel Saarinen (1873–1950), Eero grew up in Bloomfield, Michigan, where his father taught at the Cranbrook Academy of Art. Saarinen, Jr., received his art training in Paris, and his architectural training at Yale University. He worked with his father until the latter's death in 1950. He first became famous, however, for a project that he designed not with his father, but with his good Cranbrook friend Charles Eames—a chair design submitted for the "Organic Design in Home Furnishings" competition organized by MoMA New York in 1940. Their design won the first prize and led to the creation of the famous Womb Chair, which was produced by Knoll in 1948. Knoll was also the producer of Saarinen's Tulip Chair (1956).

As an architect, Saarinen became known as the designer of some important corporate headquarters, including the General Motors Technical Center, in Warren, Michigan (1956), and the John Deere Company in Moline, Illinois (1964). Saarinen's buildings could be very sculptural in appearance, as can be seen in the TWA Terminal at J. F. Kennedy Airport.
Peter Dormer, *The Illustrated Dictionary of Twentieth Century Designers* (London: Quarto, 1991), p.200.
Eeva-Liisa Pelkonen and Donald Albrecht (eds), *Eero Saarinen: Shaping the Future* (New Haven: Yale University Press, 2006).

PETER SCHLUMBOHM
(Germany, 1896–1962, USA)
Schlumbohm came to America in 1935 after having received a doctorate in chemistry from the University of Berlin. He was a prolific inventor and became famous for his Chemex coffee-maker (1941), which is still in production.
John Pile, *Dictionary of 20th-Century Design* (n.p.: John Pile and Roundtable, 1990), pp.238–9.

SKIDMORE, OWINGS & MERRILL
(Founded in Chicago in 1936)
Skidmore, Owings & Merrill has for decades been one of the largest architectural firms in the world. It was founded in Chicago in 1936 by Louis Skidmore (1897–1962) and Nathan Owings (1903–84). One year later, they opened a second office in New York. John Merrill (1896–1975) joined the firm in 1939.

The firm has been responsible for the design of some of the most prominent buildings in post-World War II architectural history, including Lever House in New York City (1952), the John Hancock Center in Chicago (1969), and the Sears Tower (now Willis Tower), also in Chicago (1973). Some of the firm's best-known architects are Gordon Bunshaft (1909–90) and Bruce Graham (1925–2010).
Carol H. Krinsky, *Gordon Bunshaft of Skidmore, Owings & Merrill* (New York: Architectural History Foundation; Cambridge, MA: MIT Press, 1988).
Bruce Graham, *Bruce Graham of SOM* (New York: Rizzoli, 1989).
Nicholas Adams, *Skidmore, Owings & Merrill: SOM since 1936* (Milan: Electa Architecture, 2007).

ETTORE SOTTSASS
(Austria, 1917–2007, Italy)
Sottsass's work spanned an astoundingly diverse range: from interior design to ceramics to product design for the Italian office equipment manufacturer Olivetti. Contrary to the dominant chic Italian design aesthetics of a designer like Marcello Nizzoli or the rationalist German aesthetics represented by Dieter Rams' work, Sottsass in the 1960s introduced the concept of "anti-design." Drawing from pop culture and *arte povera*, Sottsass mixed historical references and challenged notions of design and mass production. Defying pure modernism, Sottsass declared that design changes as societies and cultures change, and vice versa, and that a pleasing form is as important as a form that perfectly expresses the function of the product. His colorful design approach is seen in his work for Memphis, a design co-operative that influenced design across the world in the 1980s, and for Studio Alchimia, famous for its vibrantly patterned and eclectic furniture. It is also evident in the eye-catching, bright red Valentine portable typewriter he designed with Perry King for Olivetti (1969).
Peter Dormer, *The Illustrated Dictionary of Twentieth Century Designers* (London: Quarto, 1991), p.213.
Barbara Radice, *Ettore Sottsass: a Critical Biography* (New York: Rizzoli, 1993).
Ronald T. Labaco, *Ettore Sottsass: Architect and Designer* (London and New York: Merrell Publishers in association with LA County Museum of Art, 2006).

EZRA STOLLER
(USA, 1915–2004)
Stoller studied architecture and industrial design at New York University. After a short collaboration with the photographer Paul Strand in the Office of Emergency Management, he joined the US Army in 1942 and worked as a photographer at the Army Signal Corps Photo Center. Over time he developed specialties in industrial and scientific photography, but his firm, known as Esto, became best known for architectural photography. Among the many architects whose work he documented were Frank Lloyd Wright, I. M. Pei, and Marcel Breuer.
"Biography - Ezra Stoller," Ezra Stoller, http://ezrastoller.com/biography.

LADISLAV SUTNAR
(Czech Republic, 1897–1976, USA)
Ladislav Sutnar received his training in Prague and became well known for his graphic and exhibition design work. In 1939, Sutnar came to New York to work on the exhibition for Czechoslovakia at the New York World's Fair. When that show was canceled by the Nazis, he decided to stay in New York. He became an art director at Sweet's Catalog Services (a producer and distributor of product and manufacturing catalogs for the building trade) in 1941. Here, together with his colleague Knud Lønberg Holm, he developed design principles, influenced by European modernist art, that allowed them to efficiently communicate large amounts of information to the users of the catalogs. Sutnar stayed with Sweet's until 1960. He also wrote influential books such as *Package Design: the Force of Visual Selling* (1953) and the 1961 publication *Visual Design in Action*.
John Pile, *Dictionary of 20th-Century Design* (n.p.: John Pile and Roundtable, 1990), p.257.
Iva Janáková, *Ladislav Sutnar – Prague – New York – Design in Action* (Prague, Museum of Decorative Arts & Argo Publishers, 2003).

MASSIMO VIGNELLI
(Italy, 1931–2014, USA)
Trained as an architect in Milan and Venice, Vignelli became known primarily as a graphic designer, although he also worked in the fields of furniture, kitchenware, and interior design. Along with his wife Lella, he infused American design with European modernist sensibilities. They embarked on a number of ventures together, including the Milan-based Office of Design and Architecture, and the American firms Unimark and Vignelli Associates. Vignelli is known for the map he created in 1972 for the New York City subway as well as for his corporate identity work for American Airlines, Bloomingdale's, IBM, and Knoll. Husband and wife were committed to a comprehensive design philosophy, which entailed related activities like writing and teaching in addition to their design work.
Peter Dormer, *The Illustrated Dictionary of Twentieth Century Designers* (London: Quarto, 1991), pp.230–1.
Vignelli: from A to Z (Mulgrave, Victoria, Australia, Images Pub., 2007).

MAJOR CORPORATIONS INCLUDED IN THE EXHIBITION *CREATIVITY ON THE LINE*

ROSE LACHMAN

BELL TELEPHONE LABORATORIES

(American, established Murray Hill, NJ, 1925)
Bell Laboratories (Bell Labs), formerly AT&T Bell Laboratories, Inc., the research and development division of the American Telephone and Telegraph Company (AT&T), was spun off from AT&T in 1996, when that company was split into a number of smaller companies. One of them, Lucent Technologies Inc., was a manufacturer of telephone and other communications equipment, while AT&T confined itself mostly to telephone services. Bell Labs merged with Alcatel in 2006. The most recent consolidation took place in 2016, when Nokia acquired Alcatel-Lucent.

Since its founding, the organization has been on the forefront of scientific innovation, creating not only the first synchronous sound motion picture system (1926) and the first transistor (1956) but also developing research into cosmic microwave background radiation (1960s) and sonar, lasers and solar cells. Bell Labs is known as one of the most influential research centers in the world.

Arthur J. Pulos, *The American Design Adventure, 1940–1975* (Cambridge, MA, and London: MIT Press, 1988), p.309.
"Bell Laboratories," *Encyclopaedia Britannica Online*, www.britannica.com/topic/Bell-Laboratories.
John Gertner, "Innovation and the Bell Labs Miracle," *New York Times*, February 25, 2012, www.nytimes.com/2012/02/26/opinion/sunday/innovation-and-the-bell-labs-miracle.html.

BRAUN

(German, established Frankfurt, 1921)
Max Braun (1883–1951), a mechanical engineer, founded a small workplace in 1921 and invented an apparatus (called Trumpf) to fix and cut belts for machinery. Building on his success, two years later he experimented with crystals used in radio technology. Thanks to this invention, listeners could easily tune in to radio stations by rotating the crystal cylinder. The business was so successful that Braun began adding new products such as motors and pickups for turntables, portable radios, two-way radios and radio-control devices. After World War II, he explored new innovations and developed two new product categories, the electric dry shaver and kitchen appliances such as the blender (Multimix). Braun's two sons, Artur and Erwin, took over the firm upon their father's death in 1951. The brothers expanded the product line and moved the headquarters to Kronberg. In 1967, the Gillette Company bought a majority share of Braun, after which the latter company continued to sell off less profitable divisions. Braun's parent company, Gillette, was acquired by Procter & Gamble in 2007.

In 1956, Braun created its first design department, headed by Dr. Fritz Eichler, an art historian and set designer. Braun's best-known products were designed by Hans Gugelot and Dieter Rams.
"Hans Gugelot," in: *Art Directory: Design*, www.hans-gugelot.com.
Sophie Lovell, *Dieter Rams: As Little Design as Possible* (London and New York, Phaidon, 2011).

BREVETTI ROBBIATI

(Italian, established Milan, 1946)
The Brevetti Robbiati company was founded by Giordano Robbiati to produce a new type of coffee maker, the so-called "Atomic coffee machine." The coffee maker existed both as a stove-top device and in an electrical version. It was made from a one-cast piece of aluminum with some copper. The "Atomic" was also trademarked by three other manufacturers: Desider Stern was the trademark holder in Austria; in Hungary, Stern's brother-in-law produced the Atomic in his factory, Qualital; and in the United Kingdom, the Sassoon Company designed its own unique version. One of the first household items to cross the line from functionality to objet d'art, the "Atomic" is featured in many books on twentieth-century design. It was manufactured until 1985 and has become an icon of design.
"Atomic coffee machine," *Wikipedia*, http://en.wikipedia.org/wiki/Atomic_coffee_machine.

CATERPILLAR TRACTOR COMPANY

(American, established Peoria, IL, 1925)
In 1925, the C. L. Best Gas Tractor Co. and the Holt Manufacturing Co. merged to form Caterpillar Tractor Company and become the leading tractor builder of that time. Benjamin Holt, one of several brothers in the Holt Manufacturing Co., had invented the familiar "caterpillar" tractor in about 1906.

In 1986, the company was renamed Caterpillar Inc. It is still one of the world's largest manufacturers of earth-moving machinery including tractors, trucks, graders, excavators, etc., used in construction, mining, and forestry industries.
William L. Naumann, *The Story of Caterpillar Tractor Co.* (New York, Downington, Princeton, Portland, The Newcomen Society in North America, 1977, passim.).
"Caterpillar Inc.," *Gale Encyclopedia of U.S. Economic History*, ed. Thomas Carson and Mary Bonk (Detroit: Gale, 1999).
Wallace Ross and David E. Salamie, "Caterpillar Inc.," *International Directory of Company Histories* (Detroit: St James Press, 2004), pp.93–9.

CHEMEX CORP.

(American, established Chicopee, MA, 1941)
The Chemex Corporation was founded by the German-American chemist Dr. Peter Schlumbohm, who in 1939 patented a proposal for a glass coffee pot with filter, all in one piece. The hourglass-shaped carafe was an immediate success, thanks to orders from Wanamakers and Macy's. During the war, the Chemex Corporation set up an arrangement with Corning Glass Works to produce the coffee pots. The Chemex carafes are still in production (although produced by a new company) and are still a huge success.
"Peter Schlumbohm," *Wikipedia*, https://en.wikipedia.org/wiki/Peter_Schlumbohm.
"Marc Harrison Papers," Hagley Museum and Library, available via findingaids.hagley.org/xtf/search?keyword=schlumbohm.

CONNECTICUT GENERAL LIFE INSURANCE COMPANY

(American, established Hartford, CT, 1865)
Founded in 1865, Connecticut General Life Insurance (CG) had grown significantly by the 1950s and decided to erect a new building near Hartford in the town of Bloomfield, Conn. "Built in 1954–1957, the headquarters, now

known as the Wilde Building (for company president, Frazar B. Wilde), was a pioneering example of an International Style suburban corporate structure designed by Gordon Bunshaft of Skidmore, Owings and Merrill" (historicbuildingsct.com).

In 1982, Connecticut General and the INA Corporation (the Insurance Company of North America) merged into a new company called CIGNA. Though a new building was proposed, preservationists acted to oppose the plans and the building is now on the National Trust for Historic Preservation's Eleven Most Endangered Historic Places listed in 2001.
"Connecticut General Life Insurance Company (1957)," www.historicbuildingsct.com/?cat=173.
Louise Mozingo, *Pastoral Capitalism: A History of Suburban Corporate Landscapes* (Cambridge, MA: MIT Press, 2011).
100 Years in Perspective: Connecticut General Life Insurance Company, 1865–1965 (Hartford, CT: Connecticut General Life Insurance Company, 1965).

CONTAINER CORPORATION OF AMERICA
(American, established Chicago, IL, 1926)
The Container Corporation of America (CCA) was founded by Walter P. Paepcke (1896–1960) when he united 14 small manufacturers of paper boxes and containers into one. CCA was an outgrowth of Paepcke's father's lumber company that built wooden shipping crates. In 1968, the company merged with Montgomery Ward and was renamed Marcor. Subsequently, it was taken over by Mobil and then Jefferson Smurfit.

As early as the 1930s the CCA was well known as a leader of corporate graphic design for its packaging, publications, logos, and advertising. In 1936, the design department was headed by Egbert Jacobson, who designed the company's logo. It was, however, Elizabeth Nitze Paepcke (1902–94) who convinced her husband to hire modern artists for the design of the company's advertising and to create a uniform design image for the corporation's factory, offices, letterhead, and trucks. The company sought out artists such as A. M. Cassandre, Jean Carlu, Gyorgy Kepes, and Herbert Matter.

Susan Black (ed.), *The First Fifty Years, 1926–1976* (Chicago: Container Corporation of America, 1976).
James Sloan Allen, *The Romance of Commerce and Culture: Capitalism, Modernism, and the Chicago-Aspen Crusade for Cultural Reform* (Chicago: University of Chicago Press, 1983).
Michele H. Bogart, *Artists, Advertising and the Borders of Art* (Chicago: University of Chicago Press, 1995), pp.260–2.

CRANE CO.
(American, established Chicago, IL, 1855)
Richard T. Crane (1832–1912) founded R. T. Crane Brass & Bell Foundry producing valves, fittings, and specialty castings. Business expanded with the need for more industrial products in America. In 1885, the company name was changed to Crane Co. During the 1920s, this company began promoting the idea of the modern bathroom and the use of decorative bathroom ensembles. Today the company provides highly engineered industrial products in four business segments: aerospace and electronics, engineered materials for the transportation industry, merchandising systems (mostly vending equipment), and systems for what is now called "fluid handling." Industries served by these segments include: chemical industries, commercial construction, food and beverage, aviation, and power generation.

Crane was one of the leading manufacturers of bathroom fixtures until 1990 when that division was sold to American Standard Brands.
Arthur J. Pulos, *The American Design Adventure, 1940–1975* (Cambridge, MA, and London: MIT Press, 1988), pp.46–7.
"Crane Co. History," www.craneco.com/Category/28/History.html.

CUMMINS
(American, established Columbus, IN, 1919)
Clessie L. Cummins, a mechanic and inventor, founded the Cummins Engine Corporation with the financial backing of William Glanton Irwin, a local banker and investor. The company was the first to see the commercial potential of the diesel engine, an unproven

engine technology invented two decades earlier by Rudolph Diesel. J. Irwin Miller, the great-nephew of W. G. Irwin, became general manager in 1934 and went on to lead the company to international prominence. At present, Cummins is involved in all aspects of design, manufacturing, distribution, and servicing of diesel and natural gas engines, electric power generation systems, and engine-related components.

The Cummins Engine Corporation persisted in its commitment to community as well as to the vision of being an innovator. In the early 1950s, J. Irwin Miller and the Cummins Foundation encouraged the authorities of Columbus, Indiana, to improve the architectural quality of the new schools and public buildings that were going to be built in the fast-growing town. He proposed that the Foundation would pay the architect's fees as long as the client chose an architect from a list provided by the Foundation. The city accepted this generous proposal, of course. As a result, the town now has one of the largest collections of buildings designed by famous architects, including the work of Eliel and Eero Saarinen, Robert Venturi, and Harry Weese.
Balthazar Korab, *Columbus, Indiana: An American Landmark* (Kalamazoo, MI: Documan Press, Ltd, 1989).
"Cummins Engine Funds Lectureship in Memory ofPaulRand,"http://news.yale.edu/1997/05/14/cummins-engine-funds-lectureship-memory-paul-rand.

DUPONT
(American, established Wilmington, DE, 1802)
DuPont Company (in full, E. I. du Pont de Nemours & Company) is a corporation active in the fields of biotechnology and the production of chemicals and pharmaceuticals. The founder, Eleuthère Irénée du Pont (1771–1834), first produced "black powder and other explosives, which remained the company's main products until the twentieth century when it began to make other chemicals. DuPont now makes a broad array of industrial chemicals, synthetic fibers, petroleum-based fuels and lubricants, pharmaceuticals, building materials, sterile and specialty

packaging materials, cosmetic ingredients, and agricultural chemicals" (*Encyclopaedia Britannica*). Some of the better-known synthetic fibers include nylon, Lucite, Teflon, Lycra, Orlon, Mylar, Kevlar, Tyvek and Dacron. A number of mergers taking place after the 1980s brought new products, such as Stainmaster carpets and genetically modified seed plants. In 2015 the company merged with former rival Dow Chemical to form DowDuPont. Its manufacturing, processing, marketing and research and development facilities are located throughout the world.

"Dupont Company," *Encyclopaedia Britannica Online*, http://britannica.com/topic/DuPont-Company.
"Dupont," *Wikipedia*, https://en.wikipedia.org/wiki/DuPont.

GENERAL FIREPROOFING COMPANY
(American, established Youngstown, OH, 1902)
General Fireproofing Company started out as a manufacturer of building materials, but as early as 1907 it began to emphasize its line of steel office furniture, producing desks, filing cabinets, safes, and aluminum chairs. During World War II, the company manufactured aircraft parts. One of the most successful chairs fabricated by General Fireproofing was the ubiquitous "40/4" stacking chair designed by David Rowland (1924–2010). The production of most of General Fireproofing's furniture was terminated in the 1970s. The company went bankrupt in 1989 and was bought by TANG Industries of Gallatin, TN.

"Past Present Future, Archives," http://pastpresentfuture.net/archives/gf.html.

HERMAN MILLER, INC.
(American, established Zeeland, MI, 1923)
In 1923, D. J. De Pree (1891–1990), his father-in-law, Herman Miller, and a few other investors bought the Star Furniture Company in Zeeland, MI. The business was renamed the Herman Miller Furniture Company and became Herman Miller, Inc., in 1960. It manufactures furniture and interior furnishings and has always been known for its innovations in design and in organizational management. By the 1930s, De Pree had become interested in how contemporary design could improve home and office furniture. To create new products he enlisted leading designers such as Isamu Noguchi, George Nelson, and Charles and Ray Eames. In the 1960s, Robert Propst, a designer working for Herman Miller, developed the open office plan with the office cubicle as its basic component. The company became a leader in ergonomics thanks to the production of the Ergon work chair, which was designed in 1976 by Bill Stumpf, and the Aeron chair designed in 1994 by Stumpf and Don Chadwick.

Herman Miller has continued to purchase other companies associated with furniture. In 2014, it acquired Design Within Reach, a leading retailer of modern furniture and lighting.

"Herman Miller, Inc.," *Encyclopaedia Britannica Online*, www.britannica.com/topic/Herman-Miller-Inc.
Hugh De Pree, *Business as Usual: the people and principles at Herman Miller* (Zeeland, MI, Herman Miller, 1986).
John R. Berry, *Herman Miller, The Purpose of Design* (New York, Rizzoli International Publications, Inc., 2009, 2nd edition).

IBM
(American, established Armonk, NY, 1911)
In 1911, three companies, the Tabulating Machine Company, the International Time Recording Company and the Computing Scale Company of America joined to become one company, the Computing Tabulating Recording Company (CTR). In 1914, Thomas J. Watson, Sr. (1874–1956) joined CTR as CEO and turned the company into a multinational entity. He changed the name of the company in 1924 to International Business Machines Corporation or IBM.

IBM began designing and manufacturing calculators in the 1930s, using the technology of their own punch-card processing equipment. By 1953, it was ready to produce its own computers. Thomas J. Watson, Jr., took over as chairman of the board in 1961 and new divisions of the company were established. It was Watson Jr. who hired architects and industrial designers to further the marketing approach of the company.

"IBM Corp.", in Jane A. Malonis, *Gale Encyclopedia of E-Commerce*, vol. 1, A-I (Detroit: Gale Group, 2002), pp.327–81.
"Good Design is Good Business-IBM," www-03.ibm.com/ibm/history/ibm100/us/en/icons/gooddesign/.
John Harwood, *The Interface: IBM and the Transformation of Corporate Design, 1945–1976* (Minneapolis and London: University of Minnesota Press, 2011), pp.5 and 40–3.
Mary Bellis, "IBM History, Profile of a Computer Manufacturing Giant," http://inventors.about.com/od/computersandinternet/a/Ibm-History.htm.

INTERNATIONAL PAPER COMPANY
(American, established Albany, NY, 1898)
International Paper (IP) came into existence as the result of a merger of 17 pulp and paper mills in 1898. During its early years, IP was the nation's largest producer of newsprint, selling its products in the United States, Argentina, Great Britain and Australia. Headquartered in Memphis, TN, the company became an industry pioneer under the leadership of Hugh Chisholm (1866–1924) who served as its president from 1898 to 1907. Milestones included the construction of the first laboratory in the American pulp and paper industry and an innovative timber harvesting system that protected young trees. Though the company concentrates on paper and lumber production, it also produces stationery, specialty newsprint, and packaging products. Today IP supplies the raw materials for factories throughout the US and abroad, and remains the largest private landowner in America.

"A Short History of International Paper," *Forest History Today* (Durham, NC, 1998), pp.29–34. www.foresthistory.org/Publications/FHT/FHT1998/IP.pdf.
"International Paper Company," *Encyclopaedia Britannica Online*, www.britannica.com/topic/international-paper-company.

JOHN DEERE COMPANY

(American, established Grand Detour, IL, 1837)
John Deere (1804–86), a blacksmith by trade, devised a new type of plow made with a steel moldboard suitable for turning prairie soil. Enlarged demand for this type of plow led Deere to increase production and he moved his company to Moline, Illinois, in 1848. The company was incorporated in 1868 as Deere & Company. Its first riding plow was introduced in 1875. In 1918, Deere bought the Waterloo Boy Tractors enterprise, and the tractor soon became the company's bestselling product. John Deere Company remains the world's largest producer and seller of farm and industrial tractors and equipment. It has also expanded to construction, forestry, and commercial equipment, as well as diesel engines and automobiles.

"John Deere Timeline & Inventions", www.deere.com/en_US/corporate/our_company/about_us/history/timeline/timeline.page?.
"John Deere's Plow: The Plow that Started it All," www.deere.com/en_US/corporate/our_company/about_us/history/john_deere_plow/john_deere_plow.page?.
Neil Dahlstrom, *The John Deere Story: A Biography of Plowmakers John & Charles Deere* (De Kalb, IL: Northern Illinois University Press, 2005).

KARTELL

(Italian, established Milan, 1949)
Kartell began as a manufacturer of auto accessories and expanded in 1963 to home furnishings. It was founded by Giulio Castelli (1920–2006) and became well known due to the work of the designer and architect Anna Castelli Ferrieri (1918–2006). The company is famous around the world for having invented the culture of plastic injection-molded furniture and interior fittings.

To expand its market, in the 1960s Kartell began teaming up with fashion houses to manufacture footwear and clothing accessories. This came about when current owner, chief executive officer and son-in-law of Castelli, Claudio Luti, took over leadership of the firm. He worked with Versace and other design companies. More recently, in 2013,

Kartell formed an alliance with Yoox for online sales ensuring worldwide distribution.
Hans Werner Holzwarth, *Kartell* (Cologne and London: Taschen, 2013).

KNOLL INC.

(American, established New York, NY, 1938)
Hans Knoll (1914–55), a German immigrant, founded his own furniture company in New York in 1938. Cranbrook-educated architect Florence Schust (b. 1917), joined that company in 1943 and married Hans in 1946. Together they founded Knoll Associates, a company that produces office and residential furniture, textiles and leather goods with a focus on modern, functional and innovative design. Florence's training with modernist leaders such as Marcel Breuer, Charles Eames, Walter Gropius, and Eero Saarinen was reflected in the company's design philosophy, which emphasized simple beauty and minimal ornamentation. The "Knoll look" came to shape the appearance of corporate offices in the 1950s and 1960s. An open office system, the Stephens System designed by Bill Stephens, was introduced in 1973.

Realizing Knoll's importance for the broad acceptance of modern design in the post-World War II period, the Musée des Arts Décoratifs in Paris organized an exhibition in 1972 devoted to the company's furniture.

The furniture industry went into decline in the late 1970s and bottomed out in the early 1980s. During that time, Knoll was bought out by General Felt Industries Inc., which took the modern design company public in 1983. It has since been sold to various other corporations.
"Hans Knoll (1914–1955)," www.immigrantentrepreneurship.org/entry.php?rec=63.
Brian Lutz, *Knoll: a modernist universe* (New York: Rizzoli International Publications, Inc., 2010).

KODAK

(American, established Rochester, NY, 1880)
Eastman Kodak Company (Kodak) was founded by photographer and inventor George Eastman (1854–1932). The company is known worldwide as the manufacturer

of pioneering inventions such as the first portable camera (1888), the Brownie (in 1900), and the first digital camera (in 1975). The company diversified its production line by also fabricating such products as slide projectors, printers, scanners, and film for motion pictures. In 2012, Eastman Kodak filed for Chapter 11 bankruptcy protection after a steady decline in profits. By 2014, it emerged as a smaller and more streamlined company focused on imaging technologies and catering primarily to businesses rather than to consumers.
Douglas Collins, *The Story of Kodak* (New York, H. N. Abrams, 1990).
Sunil R. Mahtani, MBA, "Eastman Kodak Company," in *Salem Press Encyclopedia* (2015).
"Will Burtin," *Wikipedia*, https://en.wikipedia.org/wiki/Will_Burtin.

MILLERS FALLS

(American, established Millers Falls, MA, 1868)
The Millers Falls company, which was called Millers Falls Manufacturing Co. until 1872 when it merged with the Backus Vise Co., was founded by Charles H. Amidon (1830–aft.1900), Levi J. Gunn (1830–1916) and Henry L. Pratt (1826–1900). The company manufactured not only hand-powered woodworking tools, but also precision tools and power tools, including several types of saws and boring machines.

In 1962 the company was acquired by Ingersoll-Rand Corp. and then in 1982 it was sold to the newly created Millers Falls Tool Co. headquartered in Alpha, New Jersey.

Robert W. Huxtable was an engineer at Millers Falls and developed many of the new tools at the company, especially hand tools. His younger brother, Garth Huxtable (1911–89), had formed an industrial design firm and became the primary designer for Millers Falls, and later, its sole outside designer.
Arthur J. Pulos, *The American Design Adventure, 1940–1975* (Cambridge, MA, and London: MIT Press, 1988), pp.341–2.
"Millers Falls Company," *Wikipedia*, https://en.wikipedia.org/wiki/Millers_Falls_Company.

MOBIL

(American, established as Standard Oil Company of New York (Socony), 1882)

In 1911, the US Supreme Court ordered the dissolution of John D. Rockefeller's Standard Oil Trust, resulting in the spinoff of 33 companies including Socony. By 1920, the growing automotive market inspired the product trademark Mobiloil. Mobil was created through a 1931 merger of Socony and the Vacuum Oil Company, also a spinoff industry pioneer, founded in 1866 by Matthew Ewing and Hiram Bond Everest. Both companies were refiners of crude oil. Vacuum became the leader among Standard's companies in the use of efficient marketing and sales techniques, packaging its lubricants in attractive tins and pursuing customers with a well-organized sales team. In 1966, Socony Mobil Oil Company became the Mobil Oil Corporation. Mobil continues to exist as a major brand name with gas stations, lubricants, and petrochemicals. However, in 1999 it merged with Exxon (formerly Standard Oil of New Jersey) and formed a new company, Exxon Mobil Corporation.

In the second half of the 1960s, the firm of Chermayeff, Geismar & Haviv designed Mobil's famous logo and developed a complete corporate identification program. It was built around a specifically designed alphabet and included packaging, color, poster, and sign standards to be followed throughout the world.
"Exxon Mobil Corporation," *Gale Encyclopedia of U.S. Economic History*, ed. Thomas Riggs, vol. 1 (Farmington Hills, MI: Gale, 2015, 2nd edition), pp.403–5.
A Brief History of Mobil (Fairfax, VA: Mobil Corp., 1997).

OLIVETTI S.p.A.

(Italian, established Ivrea, 1908)

The Olivetti company was founded as a typewriter manufacturer by Camillo Olivetti. It was, however, his son Adriano who made the company into the world-famous producer of office machinery. In 1959, the company purchased the Underwood Typewriter Company. That same year, in addition to producing its line of typewriters, adding machines, teleprinters, and office furniture,

Olivetti unveiled Italy's first electronic computer, the Elea 9003. The electronics division was sold to General Electric in 1964. In the 1970s and 1980s Olivetti was the biggest manufacturer for office machines in Europe. During 1978, Carlo and Franco De Benedetti acquired a stake in Olivetti, revitalizing the firm for greater efficiency, profit and company style. In 1996, Olivetti acquired a majority share in Telecom, Italia S.p.A.

Olivetti was famous for the attention it gave to design. Adriano Olivetti believed that promoting good design for the company's factories, office buildings, workers' houses, publicity, and the products manufactured by his business was the equivalent of giving back some of the profits to the employees, who already were some of the best paid metal workers in the country. In 1952, MoMA New York held an exhibition titled, "Olivetti: Design in Industry." Another major show was mounted by the Musée des Arts Décoratifs in Paris in 1969; this exhibition toured five other cities.

In 1936, Adriano Olivetti hired Giovanni Pintori to work in his company's publicity department. Pintori was the creator of the Olivetti logo and of many promotional posters.
"Olivetti S.p.A," www.referenceforbusiness.com/history2/30/Olivetti-S-p-A.html.
Sibylle Kicherer, *Olivetti, a Study of the Corporate Management of Design* (New York: Rizzoli, 1990).

OWENS-ILLINOIS

(American, established Toledo, OH, 1929)

Owens-Illinois is a glass packaging maker, producing glass containers for beverages, food products, and pharmaceuticals. Revenue is also generated from its plastic packaging operation. The company was founded in 1903 by Michael J. Owens (1859–1923), the inventor of an automatic bottle-making machine, and Edward D. Libbey (1854–1925). It was named Owens Bottle Machine Company. It merged with the Illinois Glass Company of Alton, Illinois in 1929, and the name was changed to Owens Illinois Glass Company. Following this merger, in 1935, Owens-Illinois acquired Libbey Glass Company, maker of consumer tableware. Further mergers occurred and in about 1993 Libbey Glass spun off as

Libby Inc. The trade name O-I was created in 2005; company headquarters are now in Perrysburg, OH.
"Time in a Bottle: A History of Owens-Illinois, Inc.," www.utoledo.edu/library/canaday/exhibits/oi/OIExhibit/MainPage.htm.

PEPSI COLA

(American, established New Bern, N.C. (as Brad's Drink), 1893)

Caleb Bradham (1867-1934) invented a carbonated soda at his drugstore, which he sold as Brad's Drink. In 1898, he formed a company named Pepsi-Cola after the enzyme pepsin and the kola nut that, according to some sources, were used in the original recipe. The company's first logo was created at that time. Pepsi was devastated by the high price of sugar during and immediately after World War I, and was declared bankrupt in 1923. Charles Guth, founder of the modern Pepsi Cola company and owner of the Loft candy company bought Pepsi in 1931 and moved it to New York. Several other takeovers eventually expanded the company to produce such drinks as Teem, Patio, Mountain Dew and Diet Pepsi. There was another name change in 1961 to Pepsi. In 1965, Pepsi merged with Frito-Lay to form PepsiCo.
Michele H. Bogart, *Advertising, Artists and the Borders of Art* (Chicago: University of Chicago Press, 1995), pp.284–9.
"One Hundred Full Years," *Beverage World*, January 15, 1998, p.10.
"Pepsico, Inc.," *Encyclopaedia Britannica Online*, www.britannica.com/topic/PepsiCo-Inc.

PHILCO

(American, established Philadelphia, PA, 1892)

The roots of Philco date back to 1892, when the Helios Electric Company was founded, its primary product being the storage battery. In 1906 the company's name was changed to Philadelphia Storage Battery Company, which was shortened to Philco in 1940.

Philco began making radios in 1926. Using an assembly-line manufacturing approach, the company expanded rapidly. Philco radios were notable for their economy of design, quality, and durability. The company's product line also expanded to include televisions, refrigerator-freezers, washers and dryers, phonographs, water purification systems, and the first hermetically sealed air conditioners.

Philco's profits declined rapidly in the 1950s and the company was purchased by Ford Motor Company in 1961. The Philco-Ford name survived for a while but was sold several times starting in the 1970s, first to GTE-Sylvania and then to Philips Consumer Electric Corporation. "Philco," *Wikipedia*, https://en.wikipedia.org/wiki/Philco.

POLAROID
(American, established Cambridge, MA, 1937)
George Wheelwright III (1903–2001), a Harvard physics instructor, and Edwin Land (1909–91), a former Harvard student, are credited with the founding of Polaroid. These two men developed polarizing material for no-glare car headlights and windshields, and received a patent in 1934. Kodak was the Land-Wheelwright Laboratories' first major client in the mid-1930s when it placed a large order for photographic polarizing filters that facilitated the taking of photographs in bright light. Around the same time, a friend of Edwin Land, Professor Clarence Kennedy of Smith College, came up with the label "Polaroid" for Land-Wheelwright's products and the name was adopted in 1935. The Polaroid Corporation was formed in 1937. At the 1939 World's Fair, Chrysler Corporation agreed to run a Polaroid 3D movie in its pavilion, and the public was duly impressed.

By 1948, Land had introduced the instant camera system, which allowed for the photograph to develop itself within a minute. These black-and-white images faded quickly but the process was corrected by 1963. Color film was introduced in that year and sales rose exponentially. Polaroid continued to bring new cameras to the market.

Due to adverse market conditions, Polaroid filed for Chapter 11 bankruptcy protection in 2001. During the following years, the company's principal products remained cameras, film, sunglasses, and security ID systems, as it was merged with several international companies.
Owen Edwards, "How the Polaroid Stormed

the Photographic World," *Smithsonian Magazine*, March 2012, www.smithsonianmag.com/arts-culture/how-the-polaroid-stormed-the-photographic-world-98275389/.

RCA
(American, established New York, NY, 1919)
The Radio Corporation of America (RCA) was founded as a joint effort of AT&T, General Electric (GE) and Westinghouse to research radio as a commercial venture and capitalize on the recently developed wireless radio system invented by Marconi in 1895. GE was forced to sell its stake in 1930 due to anti-trust considerations. David Sarnoff (1891–1971) was the general manager of RCA. In the 1920s, Sarnoff and RCA played a leading role in the development of the wireless communication and radio broadcasting industries, facilitating the fields of communications and popular media through the establishment of the National Broadcasting Company (NBC). In 1929, the company acquired the Victor Talking Machine Company and in 1939 developed the first experimental television set. The first black-and-white sets went on sale in 1946 and color became available four years later. Other products developed by RCA include vinyl records, the Moog electric music synthesizer, and communications satellites. GE again acquired RCA in 1986 and began to dismantle the company. Today the RCA name and consumer electronics business are owned by Thomson, a French company, while the German conglomerate Bertelsmann owns the RCA record division.
Kenneth Bilby, *The General: David Sarnoff and the Rise of the Communications Industry* (New York: Harper & Row, Publishers, 1986).
"RCA (Radio Corporation of America)," http://ethw.org/RCA_(Radio_Corporation_of_America).
"RCA Corporation," *Encyclopaedia Britannica Online*, www.britannica.com/topic/RCA-Corporation.

RESTAURANT ASSOCIATES
(American, established New York, NY, 1919)
Restaurant Associates Corporation (RA) manages restaurants and cafeterias at major cultural institutions and large companies in New York and other large east-coast cities. RA is now a subsidiary of Compass Group North America, a British conglomerate with food service operations worldwide.

RA was founded by Abraham F. Wechsler, a coffee importer and owner of Riker's Restaurant Associates, a New York chain of coffee shops (the name was later changed to Restaurant Associates). He brought in his son-in-law, Jerome Brody (1922–2001), who expanded the chain by opening food concessions in such places as Mitchell Air Force Base, an employee cafeteria at Ohrbach's Department Store, and Newark Airport. Brody also recruited Joseph H. Baum (1920–98), who had a degree in hotel administration and had managed several hotels and restaurants. It was Brody and Baum together who made RA into the food services giant that it now is.

Baum introduced a new dining concept to the RA group, the theme restaurant. La Fonda del Sol, for example, was a Latin-theme restaurant located on the ground floor of the Time and Life Building with interiors by the famous designer Alexander Girard. Another example was the Four Seasons restaurant in the new Seagram Building (1959), where Baum planned a dining facility that changed with the seasons, meaning that the menu, color scheme and plantings were replaced every three months. The industrial designer Garth Huxtable and his wife Ada Louise, who would later become famous as the architecture critic of the *New York Times*, were hired to design an entire range of tableware for the restaurant. Eighteen of the pieces they designed were subsequently selected by MoMA for its permanent collection.
Arthur J. Pulos, *The American Design Adventure, 1940–1975* (Cambridge, MA, and London: MIT Press, 1988), p.157.
"History of Restaurant Associates Corporation," *Funding Universe*, www.fundinguniverse.com/company-histories/restaurant-associates-corporation-history/.

SEAGRAM

(Canadian, established Montreal, 1928)
Seagram Company Ltd. was founded by
Samuel Bronfman in 1928 when his Montreal-
based Distillers Corp. Ltd acquired Joseph
E. Seagram & Sons, a liquor company
in Waterloo, Ontario. The new company,
named Distillers Corporation-Seagrams Ltd,
grew rapidly in spite of, or rather thanks to,
Prohibition in the US, and by the 1940s the
firm had become the largest distiller in both
Canada and the US. Edgar M. Bronfman, the
owner's son, became head of the company
in 1971 and diversified its line of products
from blended whiskies only to include such
hard-liquor drinks as Scotch, bourbon, rum,
vodka, and gin. Wine became also part of the
inventory. Edgar M. Bronfman, Jr. succeeded
his father in 1989 and sold the liquor business
in order to purchase entertainment and media
companies. By 2002, all of Seagram's assets
had been acquired by other companies.

Innovative advertising linking Seagram's
brands with consumer culture made an
enormous contribution to the company's success.
"Seagram Company Ltd.," *Encyclopaedia
Britannica Online*, www.britannica.com/topic/
Seagram-Company-Ltd.
"The Seagram Company Ltd. History" *Funding
Universe*, www.fundinguniverse.com/company-
histories/the-seagram-company-ltd-history.
Phyllis Lambert, *Building Seagram* (New Haven,
CT, and London: Yale University Press, 2013).

UPJOHN

(American, established Kalamazoo, MI, 1886)
William Erastus Upjohn, MD (1852–1932)
was both a physician and inventor, originally
working on an innovative pill-making process
for dissolving medications more readily in the
stomach. Together with his brother, Henry, he
founded the Upjohn Pill and Granule Company,
which became the Upjohn Company in 1902. It
remained a family-run business until 1995 when
Upjohn merged with Pharmacia AB of Sweden,
becoming the ninth largest pharmaceutical
firm in the world. In 2000, Pharmacia & Upjohn
merged with Monsanto and Searle and became
known as Pharmacia Corp. Following this
merger, in 2003 Pfizer Inc. took over Pharmacia.

Leonard Engel, *Medicine Makers of Kalamazoo*
(New York: McGraw-Hill, 1961).
R. Roger Remington and Robert S. P. Fripp, *Design
and Science: The Life and Work of Will Burtin*
(Aldershot, Hampshire, and Burlington, VT: Lund
Humphries, 2007).
'William E. Upjohn: Person of the Century',
Kalamazoo Public Library, www.kpl.gov/
local-history/biographies/william-upjohn.aspx.

WEAR-EVER ALUMINUM INC.

(American, established Chillicothe, OH, 1903)
Wear-Ever Aluminum Inc. was established
in 1903 as the cookware subsidiary of the
Aluminum Company of America (ALCOA).
It was sold to Wesray Products, Inc. in 1982.
Wesray, in turn, acquired Proctor-Silex, Inc.,
a manufacturer of kitchen appliances, in
1983 and various other mergers followed,
the latest being Groupe SEB, a subsidiary of
Global Home Products.

Wear-Ever aluminum-coated cookware
and small household appliances changed the
American kitchen because of their resistance
to rusting, their remarkable light weight, and
their long life expectancy, seemingly forever.
"Wearever Cookware," *Wikipedia*, https://
en.wikipedia.org/wiki/Wearever_Cookware.
"Historical Note," Marshall Johnson collection
of cookware and appliance design drawings,
Accession 2268II, Hagley Museum and Library,
available via findingaids.hagley.org/xtf/.
"Jean Otis Reinecke, FIDSA," *Industrial Designers
Society of America*, April 26, 2010,
www.idsa.org/content/jean-otis-reinecke-fidsa.

WESTINGHOUSE

(American, established Pittsburgh, PA, 1886)
George Westinghouse (1846–1914), the
inventor of a railroad breaking system using
compressed air, founded the Westinghouse
Electric Corporation in 1886 in order to
construct and install alternating-current (AC)
electrical systems. The company flourished,
went on to manufacture mechanisms for all
stages of electrical production, and developed
into one of the leading suppliers to the electrical
industry. Westinghouse became known not only
for its household appliances, but also for the
creation of radar systems, military equipment,

and nuclear reactors. It also acquired radio
and television stations, becoming a major force
in the broadcasting industry. The company's
name was changed in 1997 to the CBS
Corporation. Westinghouse ceased operation
in 1999 and was succeeded by Westinghouse
Electric Company, Westinghouse Licensing
Corporation, and Viacom.
"Westinghouse Electric Corporation,"
Encyclopedia Britannica Online, www.britannica.
com/topic/Westinghouse-Electric-Corporation.
John Harwood, *The Interface: IBM and the
Transformation of Corporate Design, 1945–1976*
(Minneapolis and London: University of Minnesota
Press, 2011), pp.221–3.

XEROX CORPORATION

(American, established Rochester, NY, 1906)
Xerox was founded as the Haloid Photographic
Company, which originally manufactured
photographic paper. This small company
led by Joseph C. Wilson (1909–71) signed
an agreement in 1946 with Chester Carlson
(1906–68), who eight years earlier had
invented the process for printing images using
an electrically charged drum and dry powder
"toner." The creation of this printing process,
called xerography, revolutionized the world
of imaging. The invention of the photocopier
dramatically changed the workplace.

The word "Xerox" was trademarked in
1948, and in 1961 the Haloid Photographic
Company changed its name to Xerox. It is
now headquartered in Norwalk, Connecticut.
Xerox products include printers, digital
presses, projectors, and scanners. At its Palo
Alto Research Center, Xerox researchers made
important contributions to the development
of the computer mouse, the personal computer,
and the Ethernet.
Charles D. Ellis, *Joe Wilson and the Creation of
Xerox* (Hoboken, NJ: John Wiley & Sons, 2006).
Sunil Mahtani, MBA, "Xerox Corporation,"
Salem Press Encyclopedia (January 2016).
"Xerox Corporation," www.u-s-history.com/pages/
h1824.html.

NOTES

INTRODUCTION

1. Misha Black, "The Designer and the Client," lecture given at the 1956 IDCA conference "Ideas on the Future of Man and Design," IDCA Records, GRI, 2007.M.7, box 3, f.4, p.4.

CLAIMING ROOM FOR CREATIVITY

1. I want to thank Greg Castillo, Jodi Roberts, and Nancy Troy for carefully reading earlier versions of this essay and for giving me valuable feedback.
2. All quotes in this paragraph come from the International Design Conference in Aspen records, 1949–2006 (IDCA) at the Getty Research Institute (GRI) in Los Angeles, acc. nr. 2007.M.7, box 7, ff. 3 and 4.
3. See Harold Rosenberg, "The Art World, Purifying Art," *New Yorker*, February 23, 1976, pp.94–8.
4. For literature about IDCA, see: James Sloan Allen, *The Romance of Commerce and Culture: Capitalism, Modernism, and the Chicago-Aspen Crusade for Cultural Reform* (Chicago: University of Chicago Press, 1983); Reyner Banham (ed.), *The Aspen Papers: Twenty Years of Design Theory from the International Design Conference in Aspen* (New York and Washington: Praeger Publishers, 1974); Martin Beck (ed.), *The Aspen Complex* (Berlin: Sternberg Press, 2012); and Alice Twemlow, "'A Guaranteed Communications Failure': Consensus Meets Conflict at the International Design Conference in Aspen, 1970–71," Chapter 2 in *Purposes, Poetics, and Publics: The Shifting Dynamics of Design Criticism in the US and UK, 1955–2007* (unpublished doctoral dissertation, London: Royal College of Art, 2013).
5. See James Sloan Allen: *The Romance*, p.114. The history of Aspen, as described in this essay, comes primarily from Allen's excellent study.
6. The Paepckes never wanted the town to become as big as it is now. They hoped it would be a nice quiet town for them and their friends and relatives. But there was of course also a commercial component involved in this rebuilding of Aspen. The Paepckes sold many of the properties they had acquired in Aspen and thus brought in "outsiders." See Allen, *The Romance*, pp.140–1. Accusations of the Paepckes' work in Aspen as being a real estate venture would also show up sometimes in the context of the Conferences. See, for example, letter from Paepcke to Russell Wright, Walter P. Paepcke Papers, box 49, f.13, Special Collections Research Center, University of Chicago Library.
7. "Herodotus on freedom of discussion. It is impossible, if no more than one opinion is uttered, to make choice of the best; a man is forced then to follow whatever advice may have been given him; but if opposite speeches are delivered, then choice can be exercised. In like manner pure gold is not recognized by itself; but when we test it along with baser ore, we perceive which is the better." Graphic design by Paul Rand, *Great Ideas of Western Man*, Container Corporation of America, portfolio 1950–1.

8. For more on the advertisement series and the relationship between CCA's ad campaign and the University of Chicago's "Great Books of the Western World" teachings, see James Sloan Allen, *The Romance*, and also Neil Harris, *Art, Design, and the Modern Corporation. The Collection of Container Corporation of America, a Gift to the National Museum of American Art* (Washington, DC: Smithsonian Institution Press, 1985), pp.29–32.
9. In September of the same year there was also a conference of photographers in Aspen, which was attended by many famous participants, including Berenice Abbott, Ansel Adams, Margaret Bourke-White, Dorothea Lange, and the photo historian Beaumont Newhall. The conference was a success in the sense that it led to the founding of the photo journal *Aperture*. The planning of a second conference (for 1952) was initiated, but it never took place.
10. Roland Marchand, *Creating the Corporate Soul: The Rise of Public Relations and Corporate Imagery in American Big Business* (Berkeley, Los Angeles, and London: University of California Press, 1998). See also David F. Noble, *America by Design: Science, Technology, and the Rise of Corporate Capitalism* (Oxford and New York: Oxford University Press, 1979), and Olivier Zunz, *Making America Corporate, 1870–1930* (Chicago, University of Chicago Press, 1990).
11. Marchand, *Creating the Corporate Soul*, pp.357–63.
12. See in this regard the excellent study of Greg Castillo, *Cold War on the Home Front, The Soft Power of Midcentury Design* (Minneapolis and London, University of Minnesota Press, 2010).
13. IDCA records, GRI, 2007.M.7, box 1, f.2.
14. See John Harwood, *The Interface: IBM and the Transformation of Corporate Design, 1945–1976* (Minneapolis and London, University of Minnesota Press, 2011), especially Chapter 1.
15. As Harwood points out, even within IBM it was not always that easy for the designers who were brought in from the outside to make sure that the in-house designers would follow their guidelines. Communication could be difficult sometimes. See Harwood, *The Interface*, pp.46–57.
16. At the same time, in spite of the efforts of corporations to create strong identities, the customers buying their products also needed guidance as to which new inventions could be trusted best. This meant that the reverse of market research, research on behalf of the consumer, became equally important. The magazine *Consumer Reports*, founded in 1936 by Consumers Union, became a strong ally for designers promoting good and affordable design.
17. Other members of the planning committee were artists and designers such as Will Burtin, Paul Rand, and Ben Shahn; businessmen such as Harley Earl, vice president of General Motors Corporation, and H. G. Knoll, president of Knoll Associates, Inc.; and curators and scholars such as Rene d'Harnoncourt, Philip Johnson, and Edgar Kaufmann, Jr. (all from the Museum of Modern Art in New York), and James S. Plaut, director of the Institute of Contemporary Art in Boston. See various documents in IDCA records, GRI, 2007.M.7, box 1, ff.1 and 2.
18. "The Importance of Design to American Industry," invitation to attend the 1951 conference, IDCA records, GRI, 2007.M.7, box 1, f.5.
19. "Committee on Plans for Design Conference," March 27, 1951, IDCA records, GRI, 2007.M.7, box 1, f.2.
20. The original plan was to only show works produced by this company, but in the spring of 1951 it was decided to add other businesses, including CCA and Johnson Wax. "Committee on Plans for Design Conference," March 27, 1951, IDCA records, GRI, 2007.M.7, box 1, f.2.

21. In addition to the IDCA records at the GRI in Los Angeles, there is an IDCA archive at the University of Illinois at Chicago, which was donated to that university by Herbert Pinzke, an early board member of IDCA. The Reyner Banham papers at the GRI (acc. # 910009) also contain extensive documentation of IDCA, as do the Paepcke papers at the University of Chicago (see note 6). See also Reyner Banham (ed.), *The Aspen Papers: Twenty Years of Design Theory from the International Design Conference in Aspen* (New York and Washington: Praeger Publishers, 1974), p.[4].
22. Banham Papers, GRI, 910009, box 19, f.5.
23. It seems as though a timid move in this direction had already been made in 1953 when Leo Lionni, the chair of that conference, sent out a mimeographed letter to potentially interested participants, stating: "This year's Conference, although under the auspices of the Aspen Institute for Humanistic Studies, which has generously offered its facilities to the Conference, is a financially self-supporting affair. Several large industrial firms ... are contributing the money to make the Conference possible and to finance the trips of some of the foreign participants." Letter of April 1953, Walter P. Paepcke Papers, box 103, f.7, Special Collections Research Center, University of Chicago Library.
24. IDCA records, GRI, 2007.M.7, box 1, f.9.
25. IDCA records, GRI, 2007.M.7, box 1, f.13
26. IDCA records, GRI, 2007.M.7, box 3, f.4.
27. IDCA records, GRI, 2007.M.7, box 3, f.4.
28. IDCA records, GRI, 2007.M.7, box 3, f.4.
29. Quoted in Kathryn B. Hiesinger, "Introduction: Design Since 1945," in *Design Since 1945* (Philadelphia: Philadelphia Museum of Art, 1983), p.xiii.
30. One may wonder how IDCA organizers had found him as he does not have a direct connection to the design world, but it is safe to assume that the Chicagoans on the board must have known Culler from his time when he was running the Education Department at the Art Institute of Chicago.
31. See "Aspen Design Conference 1960," George D. Culler Papers, SFMOMA Archives, ARCH. ADM. 004, box C2, f.22.
32. "George D. Culler," George D. Culler Papers, SFMOMA Archives, ARCH. ADM. 004, box C2, f.22.
33. Both lectures in George D. Culler Papers, SFMOMA Archives, ARCH. ADM. 004, box C2, f.25.
34. William H. Whyte, Jr., *The Organization Man* (New York: Simon and Schuster, 1956, paperback Double Anchor Books, 1957), p.6. Another book that must have been on the organizers' and speakers' minds was most probably *Parkinson's Law or the Pursuit of Progress*, by Cyril Northcote Parkinson (1957), which investigated bureaucracy in government and business. The organizers of the conference had even invited Parkinson to be the keynote speaker of the conference. However, Mr Parkinson started his presentation by wondering why he was invited and if the organizers had intended to invite another person, a designer perhaps with the same name. He then proceeded to speak about the differences between the craftsman and the designer without ever even mentioning his own study.
35. IDCA records, GRI, 2007.M.7, box 8, f.4.
36. "Summation by Dr. Reyner Banham," in *IDCA 64*, conference proceedings, p.52. IDCA records, GRI, 2007.M.7, box 11, f.8. See also: Banham, *Aspen Papers*, p.133. For a more detailed treatment of this conference, see Greg Castillo's essay in this publication.
37. "Summation by Dr. Reyner Banham," in *IDCA 64*, conference proceedings, p.52. IDCA records, GRI, 2007.M.7, box 11, f.8.
38. See again Greg Castillo's essay in this book, and Martin Beck, *The Aspen Complex*, passim.
39. Handwritten personal memoir about Aspen, page AB/1 verso, Banham Papers, GRI, 910009, box 18, f.1.
40. Robert Fabricant, "The Rapidly Disappearing Business of Design," *Wired*, December 29, 2014. www.wired.com/2014/12/disappearing-business-of-design/.

ESTABLISHMENT MODERNISM AND ITS DISCONTENTS

1. Promotional material for "Design and the American Image Abroad," Getty Research Institute, Special Collections, Reyner Banham papers (acc. # 910009), box 20, f.5.

2. William Dunaway, "Poor Subject—Poor Conference," *Aspen Times*, June 28, 1963

3. Louise S. Robbins, "The Overseas Libraries Controversy and the Freedom to Read: US Librarians and Publishers Confront Joseph McCarthy", *Libraries & Culture* 36, no.1 (Winter 2001), p.28; Kenneth Osgood, *Total Cold War: Eisenhower's Secret Propaganda Battle at Home and Abroad* (Lawrence: University of Kansas, 2006), pp.295–6; Jessica C. E. Gienow-Hecht, "American Cultural Policy in the Federal Republic of Germany, 1949–68," trans. Robert Kimberly and Rita Kimber, in *The United States and Germany in the Era of the Cold War, 1945–1990: A Handbook*, eds Detlef Junker, Philipp Gassert, Wilfried Mausbach, and David S. Morris (Cambridge: Cambridge University Press, 2004), I, p.405.

4. Reyner Banham, "Sometimes a Great Notion. . ." in Reyner Banham (ed.), *The Aspen Papers: Twenty Years of Design Theory from the International Design Conference in Aspen* (New York and Washington: Praeger, 1974), p.133.

5. The President's Committee on International Informational Activities Report to the President (a.k.a the "Jackson Committee Report"), June 30, 1953, quoted in Nicholas J. Cull, *The Cold War and the United States Information Agency: American Propaganda and Public Diplomacy, 1945–1989* (Cambridge: Cambridge University Press, 2009), p.94.

6. Cull, *The Cold War and the United States Information Agency*, pp.183, 196.

7. "Aspen Conference with a Target," unattributed magazine clipping, August 1963; Getty Research Institute, Special Collections, Reyner Banham papers (acc. # 910009), box 24, f.5.

8. Cull, *The Cold War and the United States Information Agency*, pp.103, 194.

9. "Aspen Conference with a Target."

10. "IDCA 63: A Report on the Aspen Conference," unattributed magazine clipping, Getty Research Institute, Special Collections, Reyner Banham papers (acc. # 910009), box 24, f.5.

11. Sol Stern, "A Short Account of International Student Politics and the Cold War with Particular Reference to the NSA, CIA, etc.," *Ramparts*, March 1967, pp.29–38. Braden defended the program of covert influence in an article titled "I'm Glad the CIA Is 'Immoral'," *Saturday Evening Post*, May 20, 1967, pp.10–14.

12. "IDCA 63: A Report on the Aspen Conference."

13. Cull, *The Cold War and the United States Information Agency*, p.210.

14. ibid, pp.210, 187. Hill left the USIA in 1963 to avoid a conflict of interest when NBC began airing his dramatic series *Espionage*, produced in the UK.

15. ibid, pp.208–9.

16. Cull, *The Cold War and the United States Information Agency*, p.210.

17. ibid, p.201.

18. "IDCA 63: A Report on the Aspen Conference."

19. "Murrow Furrows H'wood Brow—Criticizes 'Image' of U.S. Abroad Created by Films," *Variety*, 6 November 1961, and "H'wood asks Murrow Provide Consultant to Mirror 'Image'," *Variety*, 7 November 1961.

20. Cull, *The Cold War and the United States Information Agency*, pp.84, 185.

21. Michelle Pautz, "The Decline in Average Weekly Cinema Attendance," *Issues in Political Economy* 11 (2002), pp.54-66 (Appendix).

22. "Aspen Conference with a Target."

23. "IDCA 63: A Report on the Aspen Conference."

24. "Aspen Conference with a Target."

25. Even after East German Party leaders in 1952 built a barbed-wire fence along the West German border (at the Kremlin's behest), passage between East and West Berlin remained relatively easy, making the city a magnet for would-be socialist refugees. An internal East German passport law introduced in December 1957 complicated travel for socialist visitors to West Berlin.

26. Greg Castillo, *Cold War on the Home Front: The Soft Power of Midcentury Design* (Minneapolis: University of Minnesota Press, 2010), pp.26–8, xii, 64–71, 83–4.

27. Quoted in Osgood, *Total Cold War*, p.218.

28. Andrew James Wulf, *US International Exhibitions During the Cold War: Winning Hearts and Minds through Cultural Diplomacy* (Lanham: Rowman & Littlefield, 2015), p.58.

29. Walter L. Hixson, *Parting the Curtain: Propaganda, Culture and the Cold War, 1945–1961* (New York: St. Martin's Press, 1997), p.40.

30. Osgood, *Total Cold War*, p.77.

31. Castillo, *Cold War on the Home Front*, pp.117–22.

32. "Image Building Abroad Should Concentrate on Underdeveloped Nations: Heiskell to DC," unattributed newspaper clipping, July 22, 1963, Getty Research Institute, Special Collections, Reyner Banham papers (acc. # 910009), box 24, f.5.

33. Daniel Boorstin, *The Image: Or What Happened to the American Dream* (New York: Atheneum, 1961), p.243; quoted in Wulf, *U.S. International Exhibitions*, p.xviii.

34. "Image Building Abroad Should Concentrate on Underdeveloped Nations."

35. Frederic C. Barghoorn, *The Soviet Cultural Offensive: The Role of Cultural Diplomacy in Soviet Foreign Policy* (Princeton: Princeton University Press, 1960), p.95.

36. Gienow-Hecht, "American Cultural Policy", I, p.406.

37. Harnden quoted in magazine clipping, article title and source unidentified, Getty Research Institute, Special Collections, Reyner Banham papers (acc. # 910009), box 24, f.5.

38. Alice Twemlow, *Purposes, Poetics, and Publics: The Shifting Dynamics of Design Criticism in the US and UK, 1955–2007* (Ph.D. diss., Royal College of Art, 2013), p.197.

39. Peter Hall, "Is City Planning Obsolete?" in Conference proceedings: "Environment by Design, International Design Conference in Aspen, June 14–19, 1970," p.62.

40. Hunter S. Thompson, *The Great Shark Hunt* (New York: Simon and Schuster, 1979), pp.151–75.

41. Unsigned memo to Larry [Halprin] from within the office of Lawrence Halprin & Associates, 7 October 1969. Ecology Action Records, Bancroft Library, University of California, Berkeley, BANC MSS 88/126c Carton 4, f.41.

42. Twemlow, *Purposes, Poetics, and Publics*, pp.189–90.

43. Steven V. Roberts, "The Better Earth: A report on Ecology Action, a brash, activist, radical group fighting for a better environment," *New York Times Magazine*, March 29, 1970, p.53.

44. Gordon Ashby, interview with the author and Padma Maitland, Pt. Reyes Station, CA, November 14, 2014.

45. In interviews with the author, Gordon Ashby, Jim Campe, Chip Lord, and Sim Van der Ryn each attributed Wilson's departure from his post as editor of *Progressive Architecture* to the negative reception of "Advertisements for a Counter Culture."

46. Curtis Schreier, "Advertisements for a Counter Culture," *Progressive Architecture* 51, no.6 (June 1970), p.86.

47. Twemlow, *Purposes, Poetics, and Publics*, p.177.

48. Cliff Humphrey, "An Ecological Foundation for Environment," in Conference proceedings: "Environment by Design, International Design Conference in Aspen, June 14–19, 1970," pp.48–51.

49. Eli Noyes and Claudia Weil, *IDCA 1970*, 22 min. (New York: Cyclops Films, 1970). https://vimeo.com/59495003.

50. Walter Orr Roberts, "Man on a Changing Earth," in Conference proceedings: "Environment by Design, International Design Conference in Aspen, June 14–19, 1970," pp.71–6.

51. Paul J. Crutzen and Eugene F. Stoemer, "The 'Anthropocene'," *Global Change Newsletter* 40 (2000), pp.17–18.

52. Reyner Banham, "The Education of an Enviromentalist," in conference proceedings "Environment by Design, International Design Conference in Aspen, June 14–19, 1970," p.59.

53. ibid, p.61.

54. Jean Baudrillard, "Statement made by the French Group," in Conference proceedings: "Environment by Design, International Design Conference in Aspen, June 14–19, 1970," pp.84–5.

55. ibid.

56. *Twemlow, Purposes, Poetics, and Publics*, p.187.

57. "Resolutions," in Conference proceedings: "Environment by Design, International Design Conference in Aspen, June 14–19, 1970," p.83.

58. Twemlow, *Purposes, Poetics, and Publics*, p.197.

59. ibid, p.198.

60. ibid, p.202.

BUILDING MODERNIST BUT NOT QUITE

1. "Company Flees Madding Crowd," *BusinessWeek*, March 27, 1954, pp.53–4.

2. For a detailed discussion of the evolution of suburban corporate headquarters see Louise A. Mozingo, *Pastoral Capitalism: A History of Suburban Corporate Landscapes* (Cambridge, MA: MIT Press, 2011), pp.101–48.

3. *Strategy and Structure* (Cambridge: Harvard University Press, 1962); *Visible Hand: The Managerial Revolution in American Business* (Cambridge: Harvard University Press, 1977) and *Scale and Scope: The Dynamics of Industrial Capitalism* (Cambridge: Harvard University Press, 1990), particularly Chapters 2, 3 and Conclusion.

4. Gérard Duménil, Marc Glick, and Dominique Lévy, "The Rise of the Rate of Profit during World War II," *Review of Economics and Statistics* 75, no.2 (May 1993), pp.315–20; Robert Brenner, *The Economics of Global Turbulence: The Advanced Capitalist Economies from the Long Boom to the Long Downturn, 1945–2005* (New York: Verso, 2006).

5. "Should Management Move to the Country?" *Fortune* 46, no.6 (December 1952), p.143; L. Andrew Reinhard and Henry Hofmeister, "Modern Offices: New Trends in Office Design," *Architectural Record* 97, no.3 (March 1945), p.99; Lathrop Douglass, "New Departures in Office Building Design," *Architectural Record* 102, no.40 (October 1947), pp.119–46; "Offices Move to the Suburbs," *BusinessWeek*, March 17, 1951, pp.79–80.

6. Likewise, Chicago's first skyscraper since 1934, the Prudential Building completed in 1955, was another example of a landmark postwar downtown corporate headquarters. Carol Willis, *Form Follows Finance: Skyscrapers and Skylines in New York and Chicago* (Princeton: Princeton Architectural Press, 1995).

7. For a detailed discussion on corporate interests in leaving the center city and joining the suburbs see Mozingo, *Pastoral Capitalism*, pp.6–11, 19–44.

8. Kenneth Jackson, *Crabgrass Frontier: The Suburbanization of the United States* (New York: Oxford University Press, 1985); Robert Bruegmann, *Sprawl: A Compact History* (Chicago: University of Chicago Press, 2005); Robert Fishman, *Bourgeois Utopias* (New York: Basic Books, 1987); Mark Gottdeiner, *Planned Sprawl: Private and Public Interests in Suburbia* (Beverly Hills: Sage Publications, 1977); John R. Logan and Harvey L. Molotch, *Urban Fortunes: The Political Economy of Place* (Berkeley: University of California Press, 2007); Robert A. Beauregard, *When America Became Suburban* (Minneapolis: University of Minnesota Press, 2006).

9. Tracy B. Augur, "Decentralization: Blessing or Tragedy?" in *Planning 1948: Proceedings of the Annual National Planning Conference Held in New York City, October 11–13, 1948* (Chicago: American Society of Planning Officials, 1948); Harold Hauf, "City Planning and Civil Defense," *Architectural Record* 108, no.8 (December 1950), p.99.

10. "Should Management Move," p.168.

11. Kristin Nelson, "Labor Demand, Labor Supply and the Suburbanization of Low-Wage Office Work," in *Production, Work, and Territory*, edited by Allen J. Scott and Michael Storpor (Winchester, MA: Allen and Unwin, 1986), pp.149–71.

12. "Should Management Move," p.168.

13. Mozingo, *Pastoral Capitalism*, pp.45–86.

14. "New View of Metals," *BusinessWeek*, no.1356 (August 27, 1955), p.158

15. "Should Management Move," p.164.

16. Charles G. Mortimer, *A Fresh Chapter* (New York: General Foods, [1954]); General Foods, *GF Moving Day and You* (New York: General Foods, 1952); General Foods, "Goodbye to Subways? GF Takes Option on Site for New General Offices," *GF News Letter* 12, no.2 (February 1951), p.2; for a detailed discussion of the motivations, process, and results of the General Foods move see Mozingo, *Pastoral Capitalism*, pp.106–12.

17. James S. Duncan and Nancy G. Duncan, *Landscapes of Privilege: The Politics of the Aesthetic in an American Suburb* (New York: Routledge, 2004).

18. David Schuyler, *The New Urban Landscape: The Redefinition of City Form in Nineteenth-century America* (Baltimore: Johns Hopkins University Press, 1986).

19. Henry Hubbard and John Nolen, *Parkways and Land Values* (Cambridge, MA: Harvard University Press, 1937).

20. David A. Granley and Charles E. Jolitz, "The New General Foods Headquarters: Its Design and Construction—Part Two," *GF Technical Bulletin* 6, no.2 (June 1952), pp.2–12.

21. "Offices Move to the Suburbs," pp.79–80; Michael Mudd, "William L. Butcher: Three Decades Building Westchester," *Westchester Commerce and Industry* (January 23, 1977), H3; Milton Hoffman, "Michaelian Was There at the Beginning," *Westchester Commerce and Industry* (January 23, 1977), H4–5.

22. Hoffman, "Michaelian Was There at the Beginning," H4.

23. Architectural Forum, "Voorhees Walker Foley & Smith," *Architectural Forum* 101, no.5 (November 1954), pp.140–7; David G. Hoffman, "Eliel Saarinen and the Cranbrook Tradition in Architecture and Urban Design," in *Design in America: The Cranbrook Vision, 1925–1950*, eds Robert Judson Clark and Andrea Belloli (New York: Harry Abrams, 1983), pp.47–90.

24. General Foods, *General Foods* (White Plains, NY: General Foods, 1954); General Foods, *GF Moving Day and You*; General Foods, "We Move Our General Offices to White Plains," in *General Foods Annual Report* (White Plains, NY: General Foods, Fall 1954), pp.12–13.

25. Elizabeth James, "Why Move to White Plains?," *GF News* 15, no.5 (1954), pp.12–13.

26. For a detailed discussion of the motivations, process, and results of the Connecticut General move see Mozingo, *Pastoral Capitalism*, pp.112–19.

27. "A Dramatic New Office Building," *Fortune* 56, no.3 (September 1957), pp.164–6.

28. ibid.; "Insurance Sets a Pattern," *Architectural Forum* 107, no.3 (September 1957), pp.114–19; "Building with a Future," p.91; for the role of women in the insurance business see Barbara Baran; "Office Automation and Women's Work: The Technical Transformation of the Insurance Industry," in *High Technology, Space, and Society*, ed. Manuel Castells (Thousand Oaks, CA: Sage, 1985), pp.143–71.

29. H. M. Horner, "Introduction," in Frazar B. Wilde, *Time Out of Mind* (New York: Newcomen Society of North America, 1959), p.6; "A Dramatic New Office Building," p.165.

30. "Insurance Sets a Pattern," pp.114–19.

31. ibid.; "A Dramatic New Office Building,", pp.164–6; "Building with a Future," p.91; "For Corporate Life '57," *Newsweek* 50, no.12 (September 16, 1957), pp.114–15; "Symposium in a Symbolic Setting: Fine New Building Meets Challenge of City Crisis," *Life* 42 (October 21, 1957), pp.49–54.

32. "Insurance Sets a Pattern," p.113.

33. Connecticut General Life Insurance Corporation, *The New Highways: Challenge to the Metropolitan Region* (Hartford: Connecticut General Life Insurance Corporation, 1958).

34. "Symposium in a Symbolic Setting," pp.49–54.

35. "Insurance Sets a Pattern," p.233; "Building with a Future," p.91; Charles Moore, "Environment and Industry," *Architectural Record* 124, no.1 (July 1958), p.162.

36. "Insurance Sets a Pattern," p.127; Moore, "Environment and Industry," p.162.

37. For a detailed discussion of the motivations, process, and results of the Deere & Company move see Mozingo, *Pastoral Capitalism*, pp.119–36.

38. Wayne G. Broehl, *John Deere's Company: The Story of Deere & Company and Its Times* (New York: Doubleday, 1984), pp.607, 614–15; William Hewitt, "The Genesis of a Great Building – and of an Unusual Friendship," *AIA Journal* 56, no.19 (August 1977), pp.36–8; William A. Hewitt, "The President's Letter," *Deere & Company 1957 Annual Report* (Moline: Deere & Company, 1957); Deere & Company, *Challenge to the Architect: Deere & Company Administrative Center* (Moline: Deere & Company, 1964).

39. Hewitt, "The Genesis of a Great Building"; Deere & Company, *Challenge to the Architect*.

40. Stuart Dawson interviewed by the author, Berkeley, California, September 17, 1997; Peter Walker interviewed by the author, Berkeley, California, November 12, 1997.

41. "Moline's Biggest Bash," *BusinessWeek*, no.1816 (June 20, 1964), pp.62–4.

42. Deere & Company, *Challenge to the Architect*.

43. Mildred Reed Hall and Edward T. Hall, *The Fourth Dimension in Architecture* (Santa Fe, NM: Sunstone Press, 1975), pp.58, 61, 37; Genevieve Sorter Capowski, "Designing a Corporate Identity," *Management Review* 82, no.6 (June 1993), p.38.

44. "The New Environment: Ten Buildings That Point the Future," *Fortune* 70, no.4 (October 1964), p.138; Walter McQuade, "John Deere's Sticks of Steel," *Architectural Forum* 71, no.7 (July 1964), p.77; "Deere and Co., USA," *Architectural Design* 35, no.8 (August 1965), pp.404–9; John Jacobus, "John Deere Office Building, Moline, Illinois, USA," *Architectural Review* 137, no.819 (May 1965), pp.364–71; "Saarinen's Deere Building Opens," *Progressive Architecture* 45, no.7 (July 1964), p.64; "Offices, Moline, Illinois," *Architecture & Building News* 227, no.21 (May 1965), pp.979–84. The project won many awards including the American Institute of Architects' First Honor Award, the Architectural League of New York's Collaborative Medal of Honor, and the American Society of Landscape Architects' Honor Award.

45. Philip Herrera, "That Manhattan Exodus," *Fortune* 75, no.6 (June 1, 1967), p.144; Roger J. O'Meara, *Corporate Moves to the Suburbs: Problems and Opportunities* (New York: The Conference Board, 1972), pp.5–8, 11; Roger J. O'Meara, "Executive Suites in Suburbia," *Conference Board Record* 9, no.8 (August 1972), pp.9–10; Richard Reeves, "Loss of Major Companies Conceded by City Official," *New York Times*, February 5, 1971, p.33; Herbert E. Meyer, "Why Corporations Are on the Move," *Fortune* 93, no.5 (May 1976), pp.252–72.

46. Mudd, "William L. Butcher;" Hoffman, "Michaelian Was There at the Beginning."

47. Jory Johnson and Felice Frankel, "Pepsico, Purchase, New York," *Modern Landscape Architecture* (New York: Abbeville Press, 1991), pp.17–27; Catherine Howett, "Pepsico Reconsidered," *Landscape Architecture* 79, no.3 (April 1989), pp.82–5; PepsiCo, *Donald M. Kendall Sculpture Gardens* (Purchase, NY: Pepsico, 1997); see also Mozingo, *Pastoral Capitalism*, pp.137–9.

48. "Headquarter Offices for American Can Are a Model of Restraint," *Architectural Forum* 134, no.1 (January/February 1971), pp.28–34; "Pastoral Palazzo," *Architectural Review* 149, no.889 (March 1971), pp.137–46; "American Can Company," *AIA Journal* 59, no.5 (November 1973), pp.120–38; Ada Louise Huxtable, "It's So Peaceful in the Country," *New York Times*, January 17, 1971, D29.

49. Huxtable, "It's So Peaceful in the Country," D29.

50. "Richardson-Merrell Headquarters Wilton, Connecticut," *Architectural Record* 159, no.2 (February 1976), pp.82–5.

51. Mark B. Milstein and Stuart Hart, "Weyerhaeuser Company: The Next 100 Years" (Washington DC: World Resources Institute, 1987), http://pdf.wri.org/bell/case_1-56973-233-7_full_version_english.pdf.

52. "Weyerhaeuser Corporate Headquarters," Process; *Architecture*, no.85 (October 1989), pp.44–5; "Wide Open Spaces," *Industrial Design* 19, no.2 (March 1989), pp.37–42; Roger Montgomery, "A Building that Makes Its Own Landscape," *Architectural Forum* 136, no.2 (March 1972), pp.22–7; Peter Walker interview.

53. Mozingo, *Pastoral Capitalism*, pp.197–201.

54. Louise A. Mozingo, "Between Power and Appearance: the Enterprise Suburbs of Silicon Valley," *Infinite Suburbs* (New York: Princeton Architectural Press, in press).

DESIGN EDUCATION AT STANFORD

1. M. Kahn, "Curriculum vitae" in Kahn papers, c.1965, Stanford University Libraries Special Collections and University Archives. Unpublished.

2. L. Jackson, *Twentieth-Century Pattern Design* (New York: Princeton Architectural Press, 2002), p.116.

3. Kahn, "Curriculum vitae."

4. https://en.wikipedia.org/wiki/John_E._Arnold.

5. *Stanford Daily* 144, issue 9 (October 2, 1963), http://stanforddailyarchive.com/cgi-bin/stanford?a=d&d=stanford19631002-01.2.3#.

6. W. Kays, P. Bulkeley, and C. Pederson, Memorial resolution to Stanford University Faculty Senate (1963), https://wayback.archive-it.org/5591/20160322163321/http://historicalsociety.stanford.edu/pdfmem/ArnoldJ.pdf.

7. M. Kahn, Report of nine schools tour in Kahn papers, 1959, Stanford University Libraries Special Collections and University Archives. Unpublished.

8. *Stanford University Bulletin*, series 18, no.2 (1966), p.145, http://sul-derivatives.stanford.edu/derivative?CSNID=00002176&mediaType=application/pdf.

9. http://www.esalen.org/page/our-story.

10. J. Markoff, *What the Dormouse Said: How the Sixties Counterculture Shaped the Personal Computer Industry* (New York: Penguin Books, 2005).

11. L. Leifer, personal communication with author, July 11, 2016.

12. D. Kelley, handwritten note in Kahn papers, 1977, Stanford University Libraries Special Collections and University Archives. Unpublished.

13. [Unknown], Presentation of Master's Projects in Graphic and Product Design pamphlet in Kahn papers, 1978, Stanford University Libraries Special Collections and University Archives.

14. J. Adams, *The Building of an Engineer: Making, Teaching and Thinking* (Stanford, California: self-published/Ad Hoc Press, 2011), p.121.

15. M. Kahn, Correspondence with Robert McLean, 1964, General Motors in Kahn papers, Stanford University Libraries Special Collections and University Archives. Unpublished.

PHOTO CREDITS

ILLUSTRATIONS

1.1 © 2015 RIT Cary Graphic Arts Collection. Courtesy of The Ferenc Berko Photo Archive | berkophoto.com.

1.2 Private collection. © 2016 Artists Rights Society (ARS), New York / VG Bild-Kunst, Bonn.

1.3 Smithsonian American Art Museum, Gift of Container Corporation of America.

1.4 University Archives & Historic Collections, J. Paul Leonard Library, San Francisco State University.

1.5 Private collection. © 2016 Artists Rights Society (ARS), New York / VG Bild-Kunst, Bonn.

1.6 © CNAC/MNAM/Dist. RMN- Grand Palais / Art Resource, NY. Courtesy of International Business Machines Corporation, © 1961 International Business Machines Corporation.

1.7 © 2015 RIT Cary Graphic Arts Collection.

1.8 San Francisco Museum of Modern Art, Gift of Dung Ngo.

1.9 © 2015 RIT Cary Graphic Arts Collection. Used with permission from the Lionni Family and the Rochester Institute of Technology.

1.10 ©2015 RIT Cary Graphic Arts Collection. Courtesy of The Ferenc Berko Photo Archive | berkophoto.com.

1.11 Getty Research Institute, Los Angeles (2007.M.7). Courtesy of The Ferenc Berko Photo Archive | berkophoto.com.

1.12 Getty Research Institute, Los Angeles (2007.M.7). Courtesy of The Ferenc Berko Photo Archive | berkophoto.com.

1.13 Courtesy of Eli Noyes and Claudia Weil.

2.1 Records of the United States Information Agency; National Archive at College Park, College Park, MD. Photograph No. 306-PSD-56-22159.

2.2 Records of the United States Information Agency; National Archive at College Park, College Park, MD. Photograph No. 306-PS-55-17678.

2.3 Michael Rougier/The LIFE Picture Collection]/ Getty Images.

2.4 Ezra Stoller © Esto. All rights reserved. Courtesy of Carol Burtin Fripp.

2.5 Records of the United States Information Agency; National Archive at College Park, College Park, MD.

2.6 A/P photo.

2.7 Courtesy of Daniel Joseph Watkins and the estate of Thomas W. Benton.

2.8 Courtesy of The Bancroft Library, University of California, Berkeley. BancMSS 88/126 c, Carton 3 f.6.

2.9 Private collection.

2.10 Photo Ant Farm, courtesy of the University of California, Berkeley Art Museum and Pacific Film Archive.

2.11 Architectural Press Archive / RIBA Collections.

3.1 Courtesy of the Westchester County Historical Society.

3.2 Ezra Stoller © Esto. All rights reserved.

3.3 Ezra Stoller © Esto. All rights reserved.

3.4 Ezra Stoller © Esto. All rights reserved.

3.5 W. Eugene Smith/Black Star. Courtesy W. Eugene Smith Archive, Center for Creative Photography © 1957, 2016 The Heirs of W. Eugene Smith.

3.6 Friedman Collection Slide, Environmental Design Visual Resources Center, University of California, Berkeley.

3.7 Louise Mozingo.

3.8 Louise Mozingo.

3.9 Louise Mozingo.

3.10 Ezra Stoller © Esto. All rights reserved.

3.11 Louise Mozingo.

3.12 Louise Mozingo.

3.13 Courtesy of Kevin Roche John Dinkeloo and Associates, LLC.

3.14 Courtesy of PWP Landscape Architecture.

4.1 Matt Kahn Papers (SC1094) Dept. of Special Collections and University Archives, Stanford University Libraries, Stanford, California.

4.2 Ken Reichard / Stanford News Service.

4.3 Chuck Painter / Stanford News Service.

4.4 Chuck Painter / Stanford News Service.

4.5 Stanford University, News Service, Records (SC0122). Department of Special Collections and University Archives, Stanford University Libraries, Stanford, California.

4.6 Stanford University, News Service, Records (SC0122). Department of Special Collections and University Archives, Stanford University Libraries, Stanford, California.

COLOR PLATES

1 Digital Image © 2017 Museum Associates / LACMA. Licensed by Art Resource, NY. © 2016 Artists Rights Society (ARS), New York / HUNGART, Budapest.

2 Getty Research Institute, Los Angeles (2723-337).

3 Carl-Ernst Hinkefuss Papers. Getty Research Institute, Los Angeles (2010.M.63).

4 Carl-Ernst Hinkefuss Papers. Getty Research Institute, Los Angeles (2010.M.63).

5 Digital Image © The Museum of Modern Art/ Licensed by SCALA / Art Resource, NY.

6 San Francisco Museum of Modern Art, Accessions Committee Fund purchase.

7 University Archives & Historic Collections, J. Paul Leonard Library, San Francisco State University.

8 University Archives & Historic Collections, J. Paul Leonard Library, San Francisco State University.

9 University Archives & Historic Collections, J. Paul Leonard Library, San Francisco State University.

10 University Archives & Historic Collections, J. Paul Leonard Library, San Francisco State University.

11 Reyner Banham Papers. Getty Research Institute, Los Angeles (910009).

12 International Design Conference in Aspen Papers. Getty Research Institute, Los Angeles (2007.M.7).

13 International Design Conference in Aspen Papers. Getty Research Institute, Los Angeles (2007.M.7). Designer: James Allen Cross.

14 Private collection.

15 Reyner Banham Papers. Getty Research Institute, Los Angeles (910009).

16 International Design Conference in Aspen Papers. Getty Research Institute, Los Angeles (2007.M.7).

17 Reyner Banham Papers. Getty Research Institute, Los Angeles (910009).

18 Richard and Dion Neutra Papers, Library Special Collections, Charles E. Young Research Library, University of California Los Angeles. Courtesy of Dion Neutra, Architect.

19 Richard and Dion Neutra Papers, Library Special Collections, Charles E. Young Research Library, University of California Los Angeles. Courtesy of Dion Neutra, Architect.

20 © 2015 RIT Cary Graphic Arts Collection.

21 © 2015 RIT Cary Graphic Arts Collection.

22 © 2015 RIT Cary Graphic Arts Collection.

23 © 2016 RIT Cary Graphic Arts Collection. Reprinted with permission by Cummins, Inc.

24 © 2015 RIT Cary Graphic Arts Collection. Courtesy of Carol Burtin Fripp.

25 © 2015 RIT Cary Graphic Arts Collection. Design: Chermayeff & Geismar.

26 © 2015 RIT Cary Graphic Arts Collection. Design: Chermayeff & Geismar.

27 San Francisco Museum of Modern Art Accessions Committee Fund purchase; © Eliot Noyes Industrial Design.

28 Piraneseum, Lafayette, CA. © Kodak, 2016. Used with permission from Kodak.

29 Ezra Stoller © Esto. All rights reserved.

30 Cooper Hewitt, Smithsonian Design Museum/Matt Flynn/Art Resource, NY.

CP 31 Cooper Hewitt, Smithsonian Design Museum/Matt Flynn/ Art Resource, NY.

32 © 2015 RIT Cary Graphic Arts Collection.

33 Digital Image © 2016 Museum Associates/ LACMA. Licensed by Art Resource, NY.

34 Courtesy of Hagley Museum and Library.

35 L. Garth Huxtable Papers. Gift of Ada Louise Huxtable and L. Garth Huxtable. Getty Research Institute, Los Angeles (2013.M.2) © J. Paul Getty Trust.

36 Cooper Hewitt, Smithsonian Design Museum/Ellen McDermott/ Art Resource, NY.

37 Cooper Hewitt, Smithsonian Design Museum / Art Resource, NY. Polaroid is a trademark of PLR IP Holdings, LLC, used with permission.

38 Cooper Hewitt, Smithsonian Design Museum/Matt Flynn/ Art Resource, NY.

39 Digital Image © 2017 Museum Associates/ LACMA. Licensed by Art Resource, NY.

40 Digital Image © 2017 Museum Associates/ LACMA. Licensed by Art Resource, NY.

41 Cooper Hewitt, Smithsonian Design Museum/Art Resource, NY.

42 Digital Image © The Museum of Modern Art/ Licensed by SCALA/ Art Resource, NY.

43 Cooper Hewitt, Smithsonian Design Museum/Matt Flynn/ Art Resource, NY.

44 Cooper Hewitt, Smithsonian Design Museum/Matt Flynn/ Art Resource, NY.

45 Cooper Hewitt, Smithsonian Design Museum/Matt Flynn/ Art Resource, NY.

46 Digital Image © The Museum of Modern Art/ Licensed by SCALA/ Art Resource, NY.

47 Cooper Hewitt, Smithsonian Design Museum/Matt Flynn/ Art Resource, NY.

48 Courtesy of Hagley Museum and Library.

49 Courtesy of Hagley Museum and Library.

50 L. Garth Huxtable Papers. Gift of Ada Louise Huxtable and L. Garth Huxtable. Getty Research Institute, Los Angeles (2013.M.2). © J. Paul Getty Trust.

INDEX

Page numbers in *italics* refer to illustrations.

A

Adams, James L. "Jim" 93
AEG: *Qualität* cover 96
American Can headquarters, Connecticut 78, *78*, 83
Ameryka (magazine) 44, *44*
Ant Farm 36, 55, 56
    "Air Emergency" *56–7*
Apple 83, 93
Arbib, Richard 139
    Visionette Portable Television *122*
Arnold, John Edward *88*, 89
AT&T Bell Laboratories 65–6
    see also Bell Telephone Laboratories
Ax, Chuck: "Washington on Foreign Policy" *102*

B

Banham, Reyner 36, *38*, 42, 52, *58*, 59
Barnes and Reinecke: juicer *136*
Bass, Saul *32*, 38, 56, 139
    "John Stuart Mill on the Pursuit of Truth" *103*
Bassett, Charles 83
Battle, Lucius D. 49
Baudrillard, Jean 59
Bauhaus 23
Bayer, Herbert 23, 27, *38*, 139
    "Aspen, Colorado, 1951–52" *19*
    matchbook for Hotel Jerome *22*, 23
Beall, Lester 139
    Connecticut General Style Book 113
    logo for Caterpillar *112*
Bell Telephone Laboratories 147
    Model 500 telephone *125*
    see also AT&T Bell Laboratories
Benson, Bernard S. 16
Benton, Tom: election poster *53*
Black, Misha 12, 13, 33
Blake, Peter 36
blender (N.N.) *133*
Bonfante, Egidio 139
    poster for Olivetti Lettera 22 Typewriter *99*
Boorstin, Daniel 51
Braden, Thomas W. 44–5
Bradford, Peter: "Sewage Treatment" *108*
Brand, Stewart 59
Braun 147
Breuer, Marcel 24

Brevetti Robbiati 147
    Atomic espresso maker *135*
Bunshaft, Gordon 68
Burtin, Will *18*, 30, *32*, 139
    Kodak Pavilion, World's Fair (model) *118–19*
    logo for Upjohn *115*
    Plastics in America (exhibition, 1956) *48*

C

cameras *126*, *127*
Carlu, Jean 19, 140
Cassandre, A. M. 19
Caterpillar Tractor Company 147
    logo *112*
CCA *see* Container Corporation of America
chairs *128*, *129*
chaise longue *130–1*
Chemex Corporation 147
    coffee maker *134*
Chermayeff, Ivan 38
Chermayeff & Geismar 140
    Mobil, Corporate Identity 117
    Owens Illinois Annual Report 116
coffee makers *134*, *135*
Cohn, Roy 42
Colombo, Joe 140
    4860 side chair *129*
Connecticut General Life Insurance Company 67–73, 147–8
    headquarters *69*, *70–1*, *73*, 83
Connecticut General Style Book (Beall) *113*
Container Corporation of America (CCA), advertising 19, 148
    "Come and Get It – Out of Paperboard! . . ." *20*
    Great Ideas of Western Man series 100, *101*, *102*, *103*
    "Herodotus on freedom of discussion" 19, *21*
Crane Co. 148
    lavatory installation *132*
Cross, James: *Design and the American Image Abroad* (IDCA) *106*
Cull, Nicholas J. 49
Culler, George D. 35
Cummins 148
    poster *115*

D

Day, Robin 35
Deere & Company (later John Deere Company):
Administrative Center, Illinois 73–5, *74–5*, *76*, *77*, 83, 150
Deskey, Donald 140
detergent dispenser, dish brush, and faucet *132*
Doyle, Michael 52–4, 59
Dreyfuss, Henry 93, 140
    lavatory installation *132*
    Model 500 telephone *125*
    Polaroid cameras *126*, *127*
drill *137*
Dulles, John Foster 42
Dupont 148–9

E

Eames, Charles and Ray 140–1
    DSS plastic stacking chair *128*
Eckerstrom, Ralph 36
Ecology Action 54, *54*
Edwards, Joe 52
Eichler Homes 86
Eisenhower, Dwight D. 42, 50
Ellwood, Craig *34*
Englund, George 49
environmentalism 52–9
Esalen Institute 93

F

Field, Marshall, III 18
Fine, Paul 35
floor lamp *96*
Fuller, Richard Buckminster 30

G

General Electric 65–6
General Fireproofing Company 149
General Foods Headquarters, White Plains 62, *64–5*, 66–7, 68
General Motors 66, 93
Gienow-Hecht, Jessica 52
Gosweiler, Herbert 141
    Predicta television *121*
Gugelot, Hans 141
Gump, Richard B. 30

H

Hall, Mildred and Edward 75
Hall, Peter 52, 59
Harnden, Peter C. 49, 50-1, 52
Hélion, Jean 19
Herman Miller Inc. 149
  chaise longue *130-1*
  Panton chair *129*
Hewitt, William 73, 75
Hill, Bill 93
Hill, Charles 45
Hinkefuss, Carl-Ernst
  packaging for Kaffee Roesterei Johann
  Berger & Co. *97*
  Qualität (cover) *96*
  "WML" logo *98*
Hirsch, Joseph: "Theodore Roosevelt on the
Purpose of Government" *100*
Hollerith, Richard 141
  workstation *124*
Hovey, Dean 93
Humphrey, Cliff 54, 56
Hurlburt, Allen 51
Huxtable, Ada Louise 78
Huxtable, Garth
  computer workstation for IBM *124*
  Millers Falls drill *137*
Huxtable, L. Garth 141

I

IBM 24, 149
  computer workstation *124*
  IBM Electric advertisement *122*
  product colors 24, *25*
  Selectric Typewriter 24, *24*
IDCA (International Design Conference in
Aspen)
  1951, "Design as a Function of Management"
  23, 27-30
  1952, "Design as a Function of Management"
  30, *111*
  1953, "Design as a Function of Management"
  30
  1954, "Planning the Basis of Design" 30, *110*
  1956, "Ideas on the Future of Man and Design"
  30-5, *32*
  1957, "Human Values in Aspen" *104-5*
  1959, report *106*
  1960, "The Corporation and the Designer"
  34, 35

  1961, "Man/Problem Solver" 16
  1962, "The Environment" 36
  1963, "Design and the American Image
  Abroad" 36, *38*, 42-52, *106*
  1964, "Directions and Dilemmas" 36
  1966, "Sources and Resources of 20th Century
  Design" *107*
  1968, booklet *107*
  1970, "Environment by Design" 36, *39*, 52-9
  1971, "Paradox" 36
  1972, "Sewage Treatment" poster (Bradford)
  108
  1973, "Performance" 36
  1974, poster "Between Self & System" *109*
  and counterculture 36, 52-9
  creation 16-30
  decline 38-9
  and the image of America abroad 42-52
Imaginarium, The *92*, 93
International Paper Company 149

J

Jackson, C. D. 42, 43
Jacobson, Egbert 23, 27
Jessup, Harley 93
John Deere Company *see* Deere & Company
Johnson, Marshall 141
juicer *136*
Julius, Leslie 35

K

Kahn, Matthew Seymour 86, *86*, 89-93
Kartell 150
  4860 side chair *129*
Kelley, David 93
Kepes, Gyorgy 141-2
  "Socrates on Doing Right or Wrong" *101*
Kevin Roche John Dinkeloo Associates 78
Khrushchev, Nikita 51, *51*
King, Perry 142
  (with Sottsass) Valentine Portable
  Typewriter *123*
Kjaerholm, Poul 142
  chaise longue *130-1*
Knoll Inc. 150
Knopf, Alfred A. 30
Kodak 150
  Pavilion, World's Fair (model) *118-19*

L

Lamb, Thomas 142
  "Reversible Wedge Studies, Paint Brush
  Handles" *136*
Leifer, Larry 93
Lever House, Manhattan 65
Liebes, Dorothy 142
Lionni, Leo 142
  flyer for Olivetti "Lexikon 80" 30, *31*
Lippincott, J. Gordon 33-5, 37
Luce, Henry 72

M

McCarthy, Joseph 42, 50
McKim, Robert "Bob" 89, *89*, 92, 93
McNally, Andrew, III 27
Marcus, Stanley 27
Marshall Plan 23, 49
Masey, Jack 49
Matter, Herbert 142
  "Come and Get It—Out of Paperboard! . . ."
  20
Michaelian, Edward 67
Middleton, R. Hunter 30
Millers Falls 150
  design for drill *137*
Mobil 151
  Mobil, Corporate Identity 117
Moholy-Nagy, László 23
Molenkamp, Jan 93
Murrow, Edward R. 42, 49
Mutual Security Agency (MSA) 49
  "We're Building a Better Life" (exhibition,
  1952) 49, *50*

N

Neutra, Richard: IDCA conferences *110*, *111*
Nixon, Richard 51
Nizzoli, Marcello 143
  Lettera 22 Portable Typewriter 27, *28-9*
N.N.
  Atomic espresso maker *135*
  blender *133*
Noguchi, Isamu 68
Noyes, Eliot 24, *34*, 36, *39*, 59, 143
  IBM Selectric Typewriter 24, *24*
  Westinghouse Pavilion, World's Fair (model)
  118

O

Office of International Trade Fairs (OITF) 50
Olivetti 27–30, 39, 151
 Lettera 22 Portable Typewriter 27, *28–9*, *99*
 "Lexikon 80" *31*
 typewriter ribbons *100*
 Valentine Portable *123*
Olivetti, Adriano 27
Olivetti, Camillo 27
Olmsted, Frederick Law 66, 67
Organization Man, The (Whyte) 35
Owens-Illinois 151
 Owens Illinois Annual Report 116

P

Paepke, Elizabeth 18–19, 52
Paepke, Walter *18*, 18–24, 26, 27, 30, 39, 52
Page, Russell 78
Panton, Verner 143
 Panton chair *129*
Pap, Gyula: floor lamp *96*
Pepsi Cola 151
 Pepsi Cola Building, New York 78, *120*
 PepsiCo World Headquarters, Purchase, NY
 78, *79*
Philco 151–2
 Predicta television *121*
planned obsolescence 33–5
Plastics in America (exhibition, 1956) *48*
Polaroid 152
 cameras *126*, *127*

R

Rams, Dieter 143
Rand, Paul 24, 143
 advertisement for IBM electric typewriter *122*
 "Herodotus on freedom of discussion" 19, *21*
 IBM product colors 24, *25*
 poster for Cummins Inc. *115*
 Sources and Resources of 20th Century Design
 (IDCA) *107*
 Westinghouse Standard Style Manual 114
Rand, Ted: IDCA report *106*
Rapoport, Anatol 16
RCA 152
Reinecke, Jean O. 143
 (with Barnes) juicer *136*
Reinhardt, Ad 16
Restaurant Associates 152

Richardson-Merrell headquarters, Wilton,
Connecticut 78, *80–1*
Roberts, Walter Orr 56–9
Rockefeller, David 75
Roth, Bernard "Bernie" 93
Rudofsky, Bernard 16
Rudolph, Paul 24

S

Saarinen, Eero 24, 144
 Deere & Company Administrative Center,
 Illinois 73–5
Sasaki, Dawson, DeMay 73, 78
Schine, David 42
Schlumbohm, Peter 144
 Chemex coffee maker *134*
Seagram 153
Singh, Patwant 44, 51–2
Skidmore, Owings & Merrill 65, 68, 72, 78, 144
 Pepsi Cola Building, New York 78, *120*
Smith, W. Eugene 72, *73*
Smith-Mundt Act (1948) 42
Sottsass, Ettore 144
 (with King) Valentine Portable Typewriter *123*
Stanford, design at 86–93
Stanton, Frank 27
Stevens, George, Jr. 45
Stoller, Ezra 68, 144
 Pepsi Cola Building, New York 78, *120*
Stone, Edward Durell, Jr. 78
Stone, Edward Durell, Sr. 78
Sutnar, Ladislav 144

T

Taylor, Dr. Harold A. 16, 17
Teague, Walter D. 30
TED (Technology Entertainment Design)
conferences 38
telephone (Dreyfuss) *125*
televisions *121*, *122*
Thompson, Hunter S. 52, *53*
Tocqueville, Alexis de 83
Tremaine, Burton G. 27
typewriters
 IBM Selectric 24, *24*, *124*
 Olivetti Lettera 22 27, *28–9*, *99*
 Olivetti "Lexikon 80" *31*
 Olivetti Valentine *123*

U

United States Information Agency *see* USIA
Upjohn 153
 headquarters, Michigan 72, *72*, 83
 sketch for logo *115*
USIA (United States Information Agency)
 creation 42
 exhibitions *48*, 49–50, *50*
 films 45–9, *46–7*
 publications 42–4, *44*

V

Van der Ryn, Sim 54, *55*, 59
Vignelli, Massimo 145
Voorhees, Walker, Foley, and Smith 66, 67

W

Walker, Peter 83
Watson, Thomas, Jr. 24
Wear-Ever Aluminum Inc. 153
 juicer *136*
Westinghouse 153
 pavilion, World's Fair (model) *118*
 Westinghouse Standard Style Manual 114
Weyerhaeuser Corporation Headquarters,
Tacoma, Washington *82*, 83
Whyte William H.: *The Organization Man* 35
Wilde, Frazar B. 67, 68, 72
Wilson, Forrest 54–5
Wurman, Richard S. 38

X

Xerox Corporation 153